GEORGE D. WOFFORD

# Fatherly Advice

## BUILDING CHARACTER

*FATHERLY ADVICE ~ BUILDING CHARACTER*
Copyright © 2008 by George D. Wofford

Published by George D. Wofford
Duncan, South Carolina
Visit www.georgewofford.com

Please send questions or comments to:
Fatherlyadvice@aol.com

ISBN: 978-0-6152-1688-1

All rights reserved. No part of this publication may be reproduced, stored in a retrieval system, or transmitted in any form or by any means, electronic, mechanical, photocopy, or otherwise without the prior permission of the copyright owner.

Unless otherwise noted, all Scripture is taken from the HOLY BIBLE, NEW INTERNATIONAL VERSION®. Copyright © 1973, 1978, 1984 by International Bible Society. Used by permission of Zondervan Publishing House. All rights reserved.

*Printed in the United States of America*

*This book is dedicated to my family. You bless me every day! I am praying for you, your children, and your children's children to the sixth generation for salvation so that our family circle in heaven will be unbroken.*

# Contents

*Foreword by Dr. Henry M. Morris III* .... 9
Introduction ............................................ 11
Chapter 1: Priorities ........................... 15
Chapter 2: Faithfulness ...................... 31
Chapter 3: Patience ............................. 43
Chapter 4: Forgiveness ....................... 53
Chapter 5: Integrity ............................ 77
Chapter 6: Love .................................... 89
Chapter 7: Accountability ................. 103
Chapter 8: Leadership ....................... 119
Chapter 9: Timeless Goals ................ 131
Chapter 10: Final Thoughts ............... 141
Appendix: Grace Through Faith ........ 147
Endnotes .............................................. 151

# Foreword

*"As iron sharpens iron, so one man sharpens another."*
*- Proverbs 27:17*

---

One of the joys of reaching "a certain age" is the privilege of seeing fruit borne in the lives of others of whom you have had the delight of ministering to in years past.

This small book, packed full of sound and practical advice, tempered with the "salt" of a solid Christian witness and the "light" of godly wisdom gleaned from years of personal study of God's Word, is an absolute delight to read. Fathers of all ages and sons in every stage of life would do well to absorb its counsel and perspective.

My memories of the Wofford family are rich and full. My wife and I were serving in a small church in Spartanburg, South Carolina, during the '70s, and my two children and the Wofford's three (George among them) became something of an extended family. Rare was the Sunday that we were not at one or another's home for Sunday "dinner" (as lunch was called back then).

The bond among us grew strong as we shared both ministry and life together. I learned much from the Wofford's – how to "do" and "fix" and "be." And, perhaps, they learned from my growing knowledge of Scripture as I sought to pastor the church we shared. "Iron" was truly sharpening "iron" during those days, now come to wonderful fruition in George's family.

I am honored to write this foreword and trust that our Lord Jesus will bless this book's ministry in the years ahead.

>
> Dr. Henry M. Morris III
> Chief Executive Officer
> Institute for Creation Research
> Dallas, Texas

# Introduction

*The Lord bless you and keep you; the Lord make his face shine upon you and be gracious to you; the Lord turn his face toward you and give you peace.*
*- Numbers 6:24-26*

---

About three years before my father passed away, I read *The Gift of the Blessing* by Gary Smalley and John Trent.[1] I did not realize at the time what a true blessing this book would become to me. It touched me very deeply. Although I was loved by my parents while I was growing up, we were not a huggy, kissy family. I remember my parents kissing me goodnight until I was a young teenager; but then the hugs and kisses stopped. I guess they thought I had outgrown them by that time. (Please, don't ever stop hugging or kissing your kids, no matter what they say or how they act. They need this kind of outward, tangible demonstration of love, affection, and affirmation from you!) After reading *The Gift of the Blessing*, I made it a point to hug and kiss my father every time we visited. I was thirty-five years old, and he was sixty-six, and we were both moved in our spirits every time we embraced.

About three months before my father died, I asked him to give me a verbal blessing, much like the Old Testament fathers did with their sons. We read in

Genesis how Isaac blessed Jacob, and how Jacob blessed his sons before he died. This was the kind of blessing I wanted. Unfortunately, my father passed away before he had the opportunity to give me this type of blessing. I made myself a promise that it would be different with my own three sons – that each of them would receive a verbal blessing from me. I decided to make a video describing the strengths of each of them and giving them a word picture describing key aspects of their character. Caleb is a towering mountain with a firm foundation. His feet are planted firmly in God's Holy Word. Josh is a mighty live oak tree, whose leaves are always green, and whose roots go deep into God's Holy Word. Benjamin is a tall lighthouse, whose light and love for God shines brightly to the world. My three sons will have this as a lasting reminder, something they can listen to over and over at times when they need encouragement.

During the Christmas of 2000, my wife gave me a book entitled *Raising A Modern Day Knight* by Robert Lewis.[2] Lewis describes the importance of passing on critical elements of manhood to your sons, and the need to mark this transition from childhood to manhood with a special celebration. As my sons grew older, I took Lewis' advice and prepared a special evening in which I gave each of them my blessing. We enjoyed a meal at a nice restaurant followed by a time of games, each one teaching an important value or moral. I shared personal challenges and wrote each a poem telling them how much they blessed their mother and me. We finished with a special time of prayer in which I gave each one my verbal blessing. It was a moving evening built on a lifestyle of time spent together as a family.

I began writing this book as a private message to my three sons. In preparing for their "manhood evening," I began to think of all the things I wanted to pass on to them. As I made my outline, the thought struck me that what my sons really needed was a handbook of advice that could serve as a reference through life. Without question, the Bible is the ultimate reference book on all spiritual aspects of life. This work is not intended to be a substitute for the Bible. To the contrary, it is intended to be a book that tells of personal experiences and how God has used various people and circumstances in my life to bring me into a closer relationship with Him. It is intended to provide practical application of some fundamental biblical principles. My hope is that fathers and young men, who will someday be husbands and fathers, will benefit from this *FATHERLY ADVICE*.

# Chapter 1

# Priorities

*"I don't want to live my life, turn around, and see that I really haven't!"*
*- Josh Wofford (at age 18)*

---

A young boy approached his busy father one evening while his father was preparing a presentation for work.

"Daddy, how much money do you make in an hour?" the son asked timidly.

Without really looking up, the proud father quickly replied, "Son, I work hard, and they know they can depend on me to do a first-class job. Why, they pay me thirty dollars an hour for the job I do."

The young boy quietly slipped away to his bedroom. Ten minutes later, he emerged with a small sock full of change.

"Daddy, I emptied my piggy bank and have six dollars and ten cents – how much of your time can I buy with that?"

Could this story happen to you? Sadly, this is the case with too many fathers. They spend so much time trying to be successful at their jobs or being involved in so many other things outside their home that they have little time left for their families.

If you do not read anything else in this book, please read this: Being a good father (or a good husband for that matter) does not require you to be perfect; it requires you to be **there!** Now read that again. Being there – what a simple concept! Yet, it seems to have escaped so many fathers in this post-modern age. There is no question that we live in the busiest time since the world began. Far too often, we find fathers who spend more time on airplanes and in hotel rooms than they do throwing a football or baseball in the backyard with their sons. They spend so much time in the office that they have no time or energy to play with their children or read a good book with their families in the evenings. And when they are at home, they let television, sporting events, or golf steal the rest of the time they could have with their families.

 May I ask you a personal question? When was the last time you went camping with your family? When did you last spend one entire day doing something – anything – with your whole family? How about two hours? When did you last have a deep spiritual conversation or devotion with your wife and children? I recently heard a great analogy. Suppose you received a note in the mail that you had won a contest and would receive $86,400 in your bank account each morning, but any money left at the end of the day would be forfeited. To clarify, if you did not spend all $86,400 deposited in the morning, it would go to $0 each night; however, you would receive a new deposit of $86,400 the next morning, and this was guaranteed for the rest of your life. What would you do with that much money every day? Would you spend it frivolously on parties or cars? Would you buy a house in every major city around the world? Would you consider giving some to your friends or to the poor? Or would you send some to missionaries? *What would you do with all that money*? Well, instead of $86,400 being deposited in your bank account each day for the rest of your life, you actually have 86,400 seconds deposited into your "time account"; that is how many seconds there are in each day. And at the end of each day, it is gone – never to be recovered.

Time! We all complain that we do not have enough time to do this or that, that there just aren't enough hours in the day to do all the stuff we need to do. But the truth is that we all have twenty-four hours each day, one-hundred sixty-eight hours each week, eight thousand seven hundred sixty hours each year. No one has more, and no one has less. Stop! Do not read through that statement. I said no one has any more or any less time. All of us have exactly the same amount of time; it's a level playing field. You see, our real issue is not time; it's *priorities*! It's about where you choose to spend that precious time. Some choose to wrap themselves in their jobs ten, twelve, or even fifteen hours per day for six or seven days each week. They never use all of the vacation they have earned. Work is the priority of their lives. They think nothing is more important than making another dollar or making it to the top. They dream of getting that next promotion. Some spend all of their free time on the golf course or at various sporting events with their work buddies. Please understand that there is nothing wrong with working hard, playing a round of golf, or going to a football game. But we must ask ourselves the fundamental question: how much time are we giving to **those things** versus **spending time with our family?**

I am reminded of a story about a Mexican fisherman.

An American businessman was standing at the pier of a small coastal Mexican village when a little boat with just one fisherman docked. Inside the little boat were several large yellow-fin tuna. The American complimented the Mexican on the quality of his fish.

"How long did it take you to catch them," the American asked?

"Only a little while," the Mexican replied.

"Why don't you stay out longer and catch more fish," the American asked?

"Oh, I have enough to support my family's immediate needs," the Mexican said.

"But," the American then inquired, "What do you do with the rest of your time?"

The Mexican fisherman said, "I sleep late, fish a little, play with my children, take a siesta with my wife, Maria, stroll into the village each evening where I sip wine and play the guitar with my amigos. I have a full and busy life, señor."

The American scoffed, "I have a Harvard Business degree, and I can help you! You should spend more time fishing, and with the proceeds, you could buy a bigger boat, and then as you earned more money, you could buy several boats. Eventually, you would have a fleet of fishing boats. And instead of selling your catch to a middleman, you would sell directly to the consumers, eventually opening your own canning factory. You would control the product, the processing and the distribution. Of course, you would need to leave this small coastal fishing village and move to Mexico City, then Los Angeles, and eventually New York City, where you will run your expanding enterprise."

The Mexican fisherman asked, "But señor, how long will all this take?"

To which the American replied, "If you work hard, you could achieve this in only fifteen to twenty years."

"And what then, señor?" asked the Mexican.

The American laughed and said, "That's the best part. When the time is right, you would announce an IPO [Initial Public Offering] and sell your company stock to the public, becoming very rich! You would make millions."

"Millions, señor? Then what?" the Mexican asked.

The American said slowly, "Then you could retire, move to a small coastal fishing village where you would sleep late, fish a little, play with your kids, take a siesta with your wife, stroll through the village in the evenings where you could sip wine and play your guitar with your amigos..."

---

You have probably heard it said that no one comes to the end of their life wishing they had spent more time at the office or making just one more sales call. On the contrary, most men wish they had spent more time with their families. So, knowing that you only have one life to live, and that each passing day is gone forever, make sure you are using every hour focused on the right priorities. Ecclesiastes Chapter 3 says:

> *"There is a time for everything, and a season for every activity under heaven: a time to be born and a time to die, a time to plant and a time to uproot...What does a worker gain from his toil? I have seen the burden God has laid on men. He has made everything beautiful in its time. He has also set eternity in the hearts of men; yet they cannot fathom what God has done from beginning to end. I know that there is nothing better for men than to be happy and do good while they live."*

---

We were a very poor family when I was growing up, although I did not know it at the time. All of our needs were met. I remember my father keeping a glass jar in his dresser where he always put his tithe as soon as he was paid each week. He was faithful to God with his tithe, and he taught each of his children the importance of giving back to God. It was a priority to him. We never owned a new car or bought new furniture. Our vacations were not extravagant adventures to New York or Europe. I remember our family going to see the outdoor drama "Unto These Hills" in Cherokee, North Carolina. We cried together as a family when we saw Tsali and his sons give their own lives in order to win freedom for the Indians who remained in North Carolina following the terrible "Trail of Tears" march to Oklahoma in which so many Cherokee Indians died.

On other occasions, we took simple camping trips to the mountains. I remember those trips with great fondness. We enjoyed picnics down by the fast-moving Little Santeetlah River under the shade of the huge Yellow Poplar trees. We hiked mountain trails through the Joyce Kilmer Memorial Forest near Robbinsville, North Carolina. These were great family vacations. They were times of sharing – sharing values and sharing our lives. They were times we enjoyed being together as a family.

My father worked very hard making parts for the textile industry in a cast iron foundry for almost forty years, but he always had time to spend with his family and time to help others in need. We went to church every Sunday morning and evening, and most Wednesdays. He was not a perfect father, but he was a man who cared about his family, and he made sacrifices for us. He understood the important things in life, and he made these a priority.

I have tried to model my life after my father – sacrificing for my family and giving to others. I have given up opportunities for promotions that would have given me more money but would have required me to travel more and be away from my family. My wife and I were in agreement to sacrifice in order to send our three children to a Christian school. It has cost us more than $250,000 for the years our kids spent in this private school before college. But we saw it as an investment that would outlive us and pay dividends in the future generations of our family. Would you permit me to chase a rabbit trail for a moment relative to Christian schools?

Let me begin by saying that none of them are perfect. Some of our friends have argued that they did not want to shelter their kids by putting them in a Christian school; they felt their kids needed to learn how to deal with the real world sooner than later. And they believed their children needed to be in a public school to be a witness to other kids and teachers. Although I certainly respect this point of view, I would offer a different perspective. Let me ask you: would you favor lowering the age at which your son or daughter could join the military so they could be sent to war at age eight or ten? How would you feel about your son or daughter getting their driver's license at age six, eight, or ten? Your response is probably something like, "That's ridiculous!" But seriously, why is that ridiculous? You might say, "They are not old enough" or "They are not mature enough at that age."

I am reminded of the story Corrie Ten Boom told about her childhood when she read the words "sex sin" in a magazine and asked her father what that meant (*The Hiding Place*).[1]

> "'Sex,' I was pretty sure, meant whether you were a boy or a girl, and 'sin' made Tante Jans very angry, but what the two meant together, I could not imagine. And so, seated next to my father in the train compartment, I suddenly asked, 'Father, what is sex sin?' He turned to look at me, as he always did when answering a question, but to my surprise he said nothing. At last he stood up, lifted his traveling case from the rack over our heads, and set it on the floor. 'Will you carry it off the train, Corrie?' he said. I stood up and tugged at it. It was crammed with the watches and spare parts he had purchased that morning. 'It's too heavy,' I said. 'Yes,' he said. 'as it would be a pretty poor father who would ask his little girl to carry such a load. It's the same way, Corrie, with knowledge.

> Some knowledge is too heavy for children. When you are older and stronger you can bear it. For now you must trust me to carry it for you.' I was satisfied. More than satisfied – wonderfully at peace. There were answers to this and all my hard questions – for now I was content to leave them in my father's keeping."

I believe it is the same with our young children. As parents, it is our responsibility to protect them from the dangers of this world, while at the same time training them to be able to protect themselves as they grow and mature. Gary Ezzo of Growing Families International[2] says we need to build the moral warehouses of our children, giving them the "reasons why" so that in future situations, they can search their own moral warehouse and find the right answer. I believe the training and education we provided our children at home was reinforced by what they were taught at their Christian school, and it helped build a strong foundation for our children as they grew older. Could we have done it without a Christian school? Absolutely! But we did not want our children hearing mixed messages too early, or having to choose between what we as parents said and what they heard in public school. We did not want to weigh them down too early before they were ready to handle the heavy decisions.

The most important thing, fathers, is that you be there to train and guide your children, that you lead by example, and that you teach with your words *and* your actions. You have to *be there* to correct wrong teaching they may be hearing and learning from other sources. There is no substitute for the time you will spend with your family. No one and no material thing can take your place.

So if being a good father is your goal, here is one practical step you can take. Begin with keeping a journal for one month. Make sure you are honest with yourself. Every evening, write down what you did with your time during the day. Do this just as you would if you were trying to track every dollar you spend during the day. Try to capture what you did each hour. Ask questions like: how much time did I spend sleeping? Driving to and from work? How many hours was I at work? How much time did I spend watching television, reading the paper, or doing things for myself? Did I spend any time in prayer or in God's Word? How much time did I spend communicating with my wife? How much time did I spend interacting with my children? What was I doing with my family – watching television or interacting in some way which communicated how much I really cared about them?

At the end of the month, revisit your journal entries. Take another sheet of paper and make a list of tasks down the left side. These should be broad categories such as: sleep, work, travel, television, time with God, time with wife, time with kids, and so on. Beside each task, list the hours you spent.

After you have recorded the time spent on each category, make a total of the number of hours; this should be seven hundred twenty if you tracked your time for thirty days. Then divide each task total by the grand total (seven hundred twenty) and multiply by one hundred. This will result in the percent of time spent on each category.

Compare your percents for "time with God", "time with wife", and "time with kids" with your other categories. Are your priorities right, or do you need to make some changes in how you spend your time?

| Category | Time (hours) | % of Total |
|---|---|---|
| Sleep | 210 | 29.2% |
| Work | 230 | 31.9% |
| Travel | 40 | 5.6% |
| Television | 90 | 12.5% |
| Time with God | 50 | 6.9% |
| Time with wife | 30 | 4.2% |
| Time with kids | 30 | 4.2% |
| Sports | 35 | 4.8% |
| Miscellaneous | 5 | 0.7% |
| **Total** | **720** | **100.0%** |

When you come to the end of your life, will you be one of those who wished you had spent more time with your family, or will you think about all the precious memories and be thankful that you established the proper balance during your lifetime. I pray it will be the latter. Perhaps even more critical, what legacy will you leave your children? There is an old popular song, "Cat's in the Cradle"[3], with the lyrics, *"He'd grown up just like me. My boy was just like me."* Our sons will likely grow up to be just like us, for the good or for the bad. Leave them the legacy you want them to become.

I will close this chapter with a reflection on a memorable vacation our family took. Living on the east coast, one of my dreams and goals had always been to take our family on a trip out West to see some of the great National Parks. In the summer of 2003, my twins were seventeen and would be entering their senior year of High School that fall. My youngest son was thirteen and would start his last year of Middle School. I realized the "family years" were drawing to a close. We would not have many more family vacations in the summer like we did when they were little. So we began to plan a trip.

Initially, my wife and I had talked about camping a week at the Grand Canyon. But my wife had been struggling with an illness for many years and did not feel she would be able to camp that long. As we set camping aside and resigned ourselves to staying in hotels, I decided I would look at other National Parks in the area of the Grand Canyon. As I began to look at the map, a much bigger picture began to form in my mind. What if we could see eight or ten National Parks instead of just one? I bought a Rand-McNally Trip Planner computer program and began to detail possible routes, and in three days, I had a plan (not surprising to my three boys).

On June 6, 2003, we began. We left Spartanburg, South Carolina, in a rented fifteen-passenger van, with our three children and my wife's parents. In twenty-two days, we saw the Petrified Forest and the Grand Canyon; we hiked to the bottom of Bryce Canyon, and climbed to the top of Angel's Landing in Zion Canyon; we saw the unbelievable giant Sequoia trees in Yosemite, and we hiked to the top of Vernal and Nevada Falls there. We spent a day in San Francisco, and then saw the Redwood forests of Northern California. We visited Mount St. Helens and Mount Rainier in Washington State. We drove through Glacier National Park in Montana all the way to the Canadian border. We saw the American bison and the geysers in Yellowstone. We were awed by the sculptures on Mount Rushmore. We visited the Little Bighorn and the Badlands of South Dakota. We made a college visit in Ohio, and our last stop was visiting friends in Columbus. I could write so many other wonderful things about this trip. It was a ten thousand mile drive that I would love to do again — but I know I will never get to do it again *with our family*. I do not believe there was a harsh word spoken during the entire trip. It was a family time. It was not the first time or the only time I had spent with our family. It was a wonderful trip, but it was built on a pattern of spending time with them, day after day, week after week, and year after year. Many seventeen-year-olds would not want to take a long trip (or even a short one) with their parents. But if there is a close bond, a pattern of time spent together, then the relationship is strong. I once heard it said that peer pressure is only as strong as a family bond is weak.[4] The challenge is to make sure you are building strong, healthy family bonds, and you can only do this as you make your family a priority and spend time with them.

Henry B. Eyring said: "Time passes at a fixed rate, and we can't store it. You can just decide what to do with it – or not do with it... Time is the property we inherit from God, along with the power to choose what we will do with it...Your inheritance is time. It is capital far more precious than any lands or houses you will ever get. Spend it foolishly, and you will bankrupt yourself and cheapen the inheritance of those who follow you. Invest it wisely, and you will bless generations to come."[5]

---

*Father God, I pray for the one who is reading this, that You would help this person to be honest with himself about how he spends his time. Forgive us for being poor stewards of the time You have given us. Forgive us for selfishly spending excessive time satisfying our own desires. And Lord, I pray that You would help each person reading this to see Your priorities during this moment in their life. Father, I pray that You will listen to the commitments that are being made right now, and that You will help that person with their new commitments. Will You help them manage their time, balance the different needs placed on the precious time You have given them, and provide them with wisdom. Help them say no when they need to say no and to always say yes to Your calling. In Jesus' name I pray. Amen.*

## Questions to Ponder

1) What are your priorities?

2) Have your priorities changed over time? Have you become more involved with work, exercise, hobbies, or something else over the past few years? Why?

3) Do you see a need to change any of your current priorities? Would your wife agree? Would your children agree? Are you willing to ask them?

4) What have been the consequences of your decisions regarding your priorities in the past?

5) What specific steps will you take to change your priorities?

Chapter 2

# Faithfulness

*"The fruit of the Spirit is love, joy, peace, patience, kindness, goodness, faithfulness, gentleness, and self-control. Against such things there is no law."*
*- Galatians 5:22-23*

---

What do you think of when you hear the word faithful? Some people immediately think of a pet. Some men might say they have a faithful dog, always ready to please, always at their side. We had several hunting dogs when I was growing up. My father loved to rabbit hunt, so we kept beagles and basset hounds. He would tell you that these dogs were faithful; they always came when he called them, and he could depend on them to track a rabbit and follow the trail until he called them back.

Some people think of their car when they hear the term faithful. I work with a guy who drives a car that is at least twenty-five years old. The paint job is faded; there are a few rust spots beginning to show up, and the upholstery is worn.

So I asked him one day, "Why don't you buy a newer car?"

His reply was straightforward: "Those newer cars are all computerized with sensors and gadgets. When something goes wrong with one of those cars, it costs a fortune to fix. I like a car that is simple and easy to work on. The car I drive has been faithful to me, and I plan on driving it until the wheels fall off." He considers his car to be his most faithful friend.

During our great family trip out West in 2003, we spent several days in Yellowstone National Park. Yellowstone was full of beautiful wildlife like American bison, elk, moose, deer, and bear. But the one thing most people want to see when they go to Yellowstone is "Old Faithful", the geyser. When it erupts, it spews hot water more than one hundred feet into the air. The eruptions last from ninety seconds to five minutes. Old Faithful got its name because you can always depend on it erupting on a set schedule. When you arrive, there is a notice showing exactly when the next eruption will occur so you can plan your day through the park in time to be back for one of those spectacular moments.

As I began to prepare for this chapter and considered my discussions with other people about the word "faithful", I wondered why people think of pets, cars, or geysers. Why do people consider things or animals or nature as being more faithful than a close friend or family member? Why is it that the last thing we think about regarding faithfulness is human relationships or our relationship with God?

Webster's Tenth Edition Collegiate dictionary defines faithful as:

> "steadfast in affection or allegiance; loyal; firm in adherence to promises or in observance of duty."

There are many aspects of faithfulness that are important. The first is being faithful to God. Do you consider yourself as characterized by being faithful to God? Don't rush through that question without giving it serious thought and a serious answer. There are so many distractions we can involve ourselves with that result in us robbing God of the love and devotion He deserves; there are many temptations along the way that, if allowed to take root, will harm that relationship.

So you might ask, "What do I do when faced with this temptation or that struggle?" I believe the key is to develop a habit of reading, studying, and memorizing God's Word! Yes, I said memorizing. Memorize key verses that will help you in your daily walk. The Bible teaches us the value of hiding God's Word in our heart – so that we will not sin against God.[1] That means we have to know it, memorize it, and mine out its truths. You may not believe that you can memorize anything anymore, but that is not true. Do you know your phone number? Do you know your address? One of the essential elements in memorization is repetition. Some people are visual learners, and they have to read or write things out in order to remember them. Others are auditory learners, and they learn best when they hear something, perhaps hearing it repeated many times, like listening to a song over and over to memorize the words.

Let me share a few practical steps you can take to get started. First, I suggest you read Kay Arthur's inductive Bible study guide, *How to Study Your Bible*.[2] This is an excellent book that identifies various stages of serious Bible study: understanding the context and setting; getting the big picture of what the author originally was teaching; determining the theme of the overall work, followed by the theme of each chapter; understanding the who, what, when where and why the book originally addressed; and doing original language word studies to get a deeper meaning of the key words in a verse. This will help you grow in your knowledge and understanding of God and His plans for your life.

Second, purchase some 3"x5" index cards and prepare them like flash cards with verses on one side and the reference on the other side. I began to seriously memorize the Bible in 2004 as a result of my older sons memorizing chapters for a Bible Quiz team they were on at school. They amazed me how quickly they could learn whole chapters and could quote them backward and forwards. I was ashamed at how little of the Bible I had memorized, so I started learning verses from our Pastor's sermon each week. This was an awesome experience because it helped to firm up in my mind the message that had been preached and how it applied in my life. As time went on, it occurred to me that I could really appreciate all the more what God was trying to tell me if I memorized an entire book or letter, so I began with the book of James, learning it verse by verse, chapter by chapter. I assure you that if I can memorize parts of the Bible, anyone can! I carried my index cards with me everywhere I went, and whenever I had a few minutes, I would work on memorizing another verse while at the same time trying to understand how the things I was learning applied to my life. The more you work at this, the easier it will become. It is really a matter of commitment and making it a priority. As I shared in the first chapter, how we spend our time reflects our true priorities. Do not allow yourself to believe the lie that you cannot memorize Scripture. You can! And as you work at it, God will help you.

Third, commit to having a daily devotional time and praying to God throughout the day. First Thessalonians 5:17 says: "Pray without ceasing." This does not mean that we should spend our entire day doing nothing except praying. It means that we are to be in a spirit of prayer and allow God to interrupt our day as He brings people to our minds those things for which we need to pray. It means carving out time during the day in which you thank Him for His blessings and ask for wisdom in the decisions you are making. It means keeping an open line in your relationship with God.

Your faithfulness to God will be challenged frequently. Perhaps it will be on your job where someone begins to tell a dirty joke, or they begin to make negative racial comments. Maybe several of your associates are listening and laughing, and you feel the peer pressure to join in. Don't do it! Be faithful to God. In the book, *In His Steps, What Would Jesus Do?*[3], Charles Sheldon's primary character, Reverend Henry Maxwell, tries to impress his congregation with his powerful sermons, but quickly learns that actions speak louder than words. Being faithful is all about our actions, not our words; it is about what we do, not what we say. James 2:14 says: *"What good is it if a man claims to have faith but has no deeds?"*

One of the Old Testament men considered faithful and righteous before God was a man named Lot.[4] In the book of Genesis, we find Lot and his family living in the town of Sodom. I cannot imagine why Lot made the choice to live there because the people were terribly wicked. Lot exposed his family and his own mind to this wickedness and corruption each day. But the Bible tells us that God saw him as righteous, and because of this, He sent angels to rescue Lot and his family from the destruction He brought on Sodom and Gomorrah. However, there was something about that place that made Lot's wife miss it. She longed to be back there. God had told Lot to take his family and run and not look back. But some fatal attraction drew Lot's wife to look back. In that moment of longing for the past, she disobeyed God's direct command, and it cost her dearly, in fact, her very life. It is essential that we maintain a close relationship with God and not allow ourselves to be drawn into the ways of the world. Christians are supposed to be *in the world*, but not *of the world*. That is why reading, studying, and memorizing God's Word must be part of our daily diet so that we can remain spiritually healthy and faithful.

King Saul was a great leader, the first king of Israel. But he was not careful to follow God's commands, and he fell to the temptation of unfaithfulness. When God commanded him to destroy the Amalekites, he decided instead to bring back the Amalekite King and the best animals from the spoils of war. When confronted with that disobedience by God's prophet Samuel, Saul was quick to shift the blame and said the people brought the animals back to sacrifice to God. But in First Samuel 15:22, Samuel asks Saul: *"Does the Lord delight in burnt offerings and sacrifices as much as in obeying the voice of the Lord? To obey is better than sacrifice...."* Because of his unfaithfulness, Saul not only gave up the royal heritage for his legacy, he irreparably damaged his relationship with God. My challenge and encouragement to you is to stay faithful to God and be obedient to His commands.

---

The second aspect of faithfulness that is critical in life is faithfulness toward your wife. In the early days of my career, I traveled with several salesmen who openly bragged about their unfaithfulness. They talked about their promiscuity as if it were some trophy they had won. It appeared there was no shame associated with the act of adultery. And this seems

# Faithfulness

even more prominent in society today. Some might even think you weird or abnormal if you have not had pre-marital sex or sex outside of marriage. But the effects of this sin of unfaithfulness are far-reaching and devastating to the family.

There was a couple at church that my wife and I were friends with. I will call them Michael and Stephanie (not their real names). During President Bill Clinton's sex scandal with Monica Lewinsky in the late 1990s, Michael was the first to criticize President Clinton for such an immoral act. A few years later, it came to light that Michael had been unfaithful to Stephanie. They separated and ultimately divorced. It was tragic. They had a fifteen-year-old son who began using foul language. His attitudes changed. His twelve-year-old sister took on bad habits of her own.

Shortly after Michael and Stephanie had separated, our family was at the beach and found ourselves staying in the same hotel as Stephanie and her two children. I was making some light conversation with the daughter at the pool and asked her what she had been doing while at the beach. Her answer shocked me. She said she had been looking for some "hot" guys. I firmly believe a twelve-year-old girl does not need to be looking for "hot" guys. They will find her soon enough! She should not even know what a "hot" guy is at that age.

The tragic influence of an unfaithful husband on the whole family can have devastating effects that will last several generations. To every man reading this, I beg you to keep your heart and mind pure from lustful thinking and actions. In First Corinthians 6:18, the apostle Paul says: *"Flee fornication."* This word fornication comes from the Greek word *"porneo,"* from which we get the English word pornographic. We need to run as fast as we can away from all forms of pornography, fornication, and adultery. In Proverbs 5, Solomon writes:

> *My son, pay attention to my wisdom, listen well to my words of insight, that you may maintain discretion and your lips may preserve knowledge. For the lips of an adulteress drip honey, and her speech is smoother than oil; but in the end she is bitter as gall, sharp as a double-edged sword. Her feet go down to death; her steps lead straight to the grave.*

My desire and your desire should be to positively influence our children and others for generations to come. This is an area that you and I alone must choose. If you are reading this as an unmarried man, I encourage you to keep yourself pure for your future wife. She deserves your faithfulness to her, even though you may not even know who she is yet. Don't you want to come to your wedding night knowing you have saved yourself for that special person with whom you will share the rest of your life? Isn't that what you want from your wife? Make that commitment today, to be faithful and not give in to the momentary self-gratification that gives birth to guilt and pain.

If you are reading this and you have already had sex outside of marriage, stop right now and ask God to forgive you. There is no sin too big for God to forgive. He loves us with unconditional love. He *can and will forgive and forget* every sin that we confess. God is a God of second chances, a God of new beginnings. So if you have been unfaithful, ask God to forgive you, and make a commitment to start anew today, never to allow yourself to be unfaithful again.

Finally, be careful with your eyes. The eyes are what allow visual temptations to enter your heart. Be careful what you watch on television. Most of the programs broadcast on television are not worth wasting time on. You would be much better off reading a book, studying the Bible, or spending that time in prayer with God. Be careful with what you see on the internet or in magazines. We are constantly pummeled with pornography and sexual temptations – from the advertisements in the mall to the billboards on the highway. Satan knows that if he can snare us with this temptation and can cause us to sin, he will be able to use that to condemn us and make us feel guilty and worthless for the rest of our lives. The Bible says in Mark 9:47 that *"if your eye causes you to sin, pluck it out."* That is not a recipe for self-mutilation but rather a charge to keep ourselves holy. We are to practice self-disciple and take control of our bodies, bringing them into obedience to God's Word. Once you allow a sinful, pornographic picture to burn itself into your mind, it is very difficult, if not impossible, to erase. I can tell you it is true in my own life, and I know it is true in the lives of other men.

I know a man who had four children. The fourth came late in his life. As the older children went off to college, the husband and wife separated. The husband told me there was no particular reason for their separation; it was just that he and his wife discovered they did not know each other after their older children left home. The man did not know that I had unexpectedly found him engrossed in a pornographic magazine a year earlier. Although I do not know for certain, I would guess this was a primary reason his marriage failed. I doubt his wife even knew it, but pornography can have that kind of devastation on a marriage. It is a cancer that grows and grows until it consumes the mind of the man who is taking it in.

The good news is God forgives us when we ask. First John 1:9 says: *"If we confess our sins, he is faithful and just and will forgive us our sins and purify us from all unrighteousness."* God gives us mercy and grace, but he expects us to stay faithful to Him. And that means guarding our eyes, our minds, and our hearts.

---

*F*ather God, I pray that You would put Your hedge of protection around the one who is reading this right now, that You would protect him physically, spiritually, mentally, and emotionally. Father, I pray You would help him to make a decision today to be faithful to You, to be faithful to his spouse, and to commit himself to do what is right, no matter how he feels. Help him see that momentary pleasure is only temporary, but it leaves a long trail of hurt and consequences that can last generations. You have always desired to have a people who were set apart – holy and righteous before You. May that be our hearts' desire, to live lives that are holy and faithful before You.

And Father, for those of us who have failed at some point in the past, we ask Your forgiveness, because You have promised that if we would confess our sins, you would forgive us and make us clean. So at this moment, we confess our past unfaithfulness, and we ask for Your forgiveness. Thank You for being a Father of second chances. Thank You for being faithful even when we are not. Now I pray that You will listen to the commitments that are being made right now, and that You will help each person fulfill their new commitments.

In Jesus' name I pray.
Amen.

## Questions to Ponder

1) How would you describe the idea of faithfulness?

2) Would you say you have been faithful to God?

3) Would you say you have been faithful to your wife or your future wife?

4) Regardless of how you answered the previous two questions, God can and will forgive you for any unfaithfulness in your life. Do you need to stop right now and ask God to forgive you for any unfaithfulness? If yes, do it now! †

5) What specifically will you do to ensure you are faithful from this day forward?

---

† If Christ is Lord of your life, and you have sincerely asked God to forgive you for your past failures, He has forgiven you. Write a date by this section so that the next time you feel guilty or unworthy, you can come back to this page and recognize Satan can no longer accuse you or make you feel guilty because God has taken all your guilt away. If you do not have a personal, intimate relationship with Jesus but would like to learn more about this, please see the Appendix: Grace Through Faith.

## Chapter 3

# Patience

*"We could never learn to be brave and patient, if there were only joy in the world."*
*- Helen Keller (1880-1968)*[1]

---

Let's be honest – most men are not very patient! In fact, in my observation, most people are not very patient. We live in an instant society. We were raised with microwave ovens so that we would not have to wait for a conventional oven to cook our meals. We expect to go through a drive-thru window and have a hot meal that tastes good handed to us in 30 seconds or less. And that has become our mentality about life. When we are sick, we expect a doctor to give us some medicine that makes us feel better in minutes, or certainly hours. We hate standing in lines at the store that makes us wait ten minutes to check out. We say things like: "I don't understand why they don't hire more people to run the registers, so they don't have such long lines." But what we really mean is: "I don't understand why they are not taking care of *my* needs faster so *I* don't have to wait – don't they know *I* am a busy person with lots of things to do?"

Patience is a lost virtue. You have probably heard of the prayer for patience that goes something like: "Lord, give me patience and give it to me now!!"

That's our mindset. We want what we want when we want it. We expect to be treated in a way that requires people to focus on us, on meeting our every desire, and we really do not care how that may affect anyone else. Now listen carefully: I want to tell you a secret about patience. This secret may surprise you, and I do not believe it is intuitive or obvious. So come in real close and let me share it with you: the secret to gaining patience is not about learning to wait; it is about practicing the first and second greatest commandment.

When Jesus was asked what the greatest commandment was in Matthew 22:37:

> *Jesus replied: "'Love the Lord your God with all your heart and with all your soul and with all your mind.' This is the first and greatest commandment. And the second is like it: 'Love your neighbor as yourself.' All of the Law and the Prophets hang on these two commandments."*

Now you may be thinking: "What does loving God or loving my neighbor have to do with me being patient?" Let's start with the second greatest commandment: "love your neighbor as yourself." Loving others is a concept of which we sometimes lose sight. This is particularly true for those "others" that are not very lovable. If I am honest, I must tell you there are some people who absolutely drive me crazy. It seems they try to frustrate me or to irritate me as if that were their sole purpose in life. It would appear as if they enjoy doing that. I am sure you probably know one or two people like that, too. But loving others means putting others' needs ahead of our own. That means waiting while the needs of someone else are being taken care of. That is patience. It also means trying to look at others through God's eyes. Remember that He loves them just like He loves you. He cares about them. They are important to Him. And you may be the only Jesus they ever see.

So being patient with others is really about showing them God's love and kindness as it is reflected by you. What kind of a God-mirror are you? Consider the fruit of the spirit from Galatians 5:22: *love, joy, peace, patience, kindness, goodness, faithfulness, gentleness and self-control.* Is this what others see when they look at you and how you live your life each day? I am not talking about how you act in church on Sundays. Is this the way others see you on Monday through Friday on the job or when things get tense or when that particular person who knows just the right buttons to push is pushing your buttons? Are you a reflection of God's patience and love during those times?

Now let's look at the greatest commandment – loving God. How does this relate to patience? The Bible says that to love God means to obey Him and His commandments. So to really love God, we have to love others, and this requires us to exercise patience. We will come back to a discussion on love in Chapter Six.

---

A few years ago, I saw a documentary on television about a housewife in Russia in which the camera crew followed her to experience her "typical day." Her husband only made enough money for her to buy one day's groceries. So each morning, she would get up early and walk a long distance to a grocery store. They only allowed a limited number of people in the store at a time, so the lines to enter were very long – usually hundreds of people. She would wait for several hours to get her turn, then finally, she could go in. But unlike stores in America, the shelves were mostly empty. There were not seventeen varieties of corn or beans to choose from. She was lucky if there was one can she could buy. She had to take whatever she could find. And when she left that store, she went to another store, only to get in line again, in order to buy bread. Then another store and another line to buy cheese. The housewife finished her day late and returned home with just enough food to prepare the evening meal, only to get up the next day and do the same routine over again. That requires patience and perseverance.

Our western mentality may have a hard time identifying with this lifestyle, but there are people all around the world who can only afford to buy enough toothpaste to brush their teeth once. Americans are tremendously wealthy compared to the rest of the world, and we take that for granted. Our wealth, along with the façade of self-sufficiency, has caused us to be less dependent on God. The end result is that we have become selfish and self-focused rather than patient or persevering.

We often go through life comparing what we have to what others have. In 1981, when my wife and I got married, we literally had less than $100 to our name. I had just finished college, and those were lean years. Interest rates on a new home were at 18%! So buying anything on credit meant you were paying a lot of interest. We could not afford to buy a house, so we rented a small house for the next three years. Our living room couch and chairs were hand-me-downs from my parents. We purchased our kitchen table and coffee table from a lady selling used furniture. Everything we had was used. Nothing we had was as nice as most of our friends' possessions, but we did not borrow any money to buy things.

We saved as the years went by and began building our first house in 1984. We had saved a reasonable nest egg in those early years of marriage before kids came along, and we borrowed the rest of the money we needed from my father. We never had a bank loan, and to this day, we have never had a bank loan for anything. We bought our first new vehicle in 1991, ten years after we were married, paying almost $20,000 cash for it because we had planned and saved for it through those early years.

It was also important to us that my wife stay home when the kids were born. This was a huge sacrifice – not only financially, it was also a sacrifice for her to dedicate herself and all of her energy to being a full-time mom. This was not an eight-hour-a-day job. It required her to be available 24/7 to meet their needs, guide them, discipline them, train them, and encourage them. We believe God blessed us with children so that **we could raise them**, not someone else – not a Day Care, not even a Church-based program.

The early years of childhood are the most formative. They are learning so quickly and parroting what they see and hear around them. Patterns of thinking and behavior that shape a person's entire life are created in the first five years of life. These are the years when a mom's role is critical. No one else will be as concerned with your child's spiritual, emotional, mental, and social well-being. In the final analysis, these early years have a significant impact on the legacy we leave behind because it molds the heart of the child, and this child will one day grow into an adult who will get married and have children of their own. So we decided before we were married that when the kids came along, mom would be at home with them. This required sacrifice and patience, but that was far more important than any material possessions or personal pleasures.

Starting out with used furniture, used cars, and without all of the luxuries some of our friends had was very hard. It required patience and discipline. But doing that kept us from going into debt. And it allowed us to begin saving for the school years, where we were able to send all three of our children to a private Christian school, as I mentioned previously. This environment reinforced the biblical principles we were trying to teach them at home. There is no doubt it required serious sacrifice, just as it did for their mom to stay home, but we saw this as an essential investment in their lives and in our future heritage. We are convinced it was the best investment we have ever made. However, it was only possible because we were patient – not having to have the newest and best of everything, particularly in our early years of marriage, where lifestyle habits were developed. As our kids grew older, we were able to take trips and do other things as a family that had lasting value, far beyond what a new car or new furniture could ever bring.

So I must ask: Do you consider yourself a patient person? How would your closest friend describe you? Do you have to have what you want, when you want it, and that is usually now? Do you always have to have the newest and best of everything? What would happen if you bought a used car instead of a new car the next time you needed another vehicle, and you began making payments to a savings account as if you had bought that new car, so that future cars could be paid off with cash rather than going into debt for them? What would happen if you made the choice not to buy anything on credit, but rather you made the decision you would go without if you could not pay cash for it?

Here is another scenario that might prove useful. Imagine that you lost your job tomorrow, and you found a new one which only paid you 60% of your previous job. How would you adjust your spending habits to compensate? When you find the answer to that question, then adopt that lifestyle for the next three to six months and save the other 40% to help pay off any debts in order to begin building that nest egg for the future.

Patience is a virtue to be sought after in life. My life's verse is Isaiah 40:31:

> *But they that wait upon the Lord shall renew their strength; they shall mount up with wings as eagles; they shall run and not be weary; and they shall walk and not faint.*[2]

Have you ever heard the expression "You have over-run your headlights"? This expression originated from the idea that a car's headlights allow you to see only a certain distance in front of you at night. If an animal were to run into your path, you should be driving at an appropriate speed to be able to stop before you hit it. If you are going too fast and cannot stop in time, it is said that you are "over-running your headlights." At times, the same can be said about how we live our lives. Instead of being patient and seeing how God is working, we over-run our headlights, and the results are catastrophic. God is our headlight. He lights our path just far enough ahead – not so far that we stop depending on Him, but just far enough to keep us moving in the right direction. He is *"a lamp to my feet, and a light for my path."*[3] Be patient and follow his leading.

What is patience? It is a choice that we make about how we will live our lives. It is about recognizing that others are made in God's image and that He loves them, so we should too. It is about putting others ahead of ourselves. Patience involves sacrificing today's wants in order to better meet tomorrow's needs and goals. It consists of living a life of balance to help us get through the rough storms of the future. James 5:7-8 says:

> *Be patient, then brothers, until the Lord's coming. See how the farmer waits for the land to yield its valuable crop and how patient he is for the autumn and spring rains. You, too, be patient and stand firm, because the Lord's coming is near.*

---

*F*ather God, I pray for patience for the one who is reading this right now. I pray You would impress on his heart that the real meaning of patience is being others-focused, and considering others' needs before his own, just as You did when You came to earth for us.

Lord, all of us struggle with patience. Perhaps those of us in America struggle more with patience than people in other parts of the world because we tend to be more selfish and self-centered.

Help each of us to become others-focused, recognizing that this is how we reflect Your nature to them. Forgive us where we have failed to be patient and where we have hurt Your name. Let us start fresh and new today committed to reflecting Your love to others through the patience we display in our daily walk.

And Father, I pray You would help us be good stewards of the resources You have entrusted to us. Help us not to fill our lives with all the stuff that commercials try to make us believe we cannot live without. Help us not be covetous of things others have, but to be content with the things You provide. Thank you for Your blessings.

In Jesus' name I pray.
Amen.

## Questions to Ponder

1) Are you generally characterized by your friends as a patient person or someone who is not very patient? Why?

2) Can you identify someone who really knows how to push your buttons – that person that makes your blood pressure go up when you hear their voice? Would you commit to pray for that person every day, and pray that God would help you be a God-mirror to them?

3) Are you living a lifestyle that is pleasing to God financially? Are you sacrificing appropriately today in order to have savings for future needs?

4) Do you spend more time thinking about the needs of others, or more time thinking about your own wants and desires?

## Chapter 4

# Forgiveness

*"When we genuinely forgive, we set a prisoner free, and then we discover that the prisoner we set free was us."*
*- Philip Yancey*
*(What's So Amazing About Grace)* [1]

---

How often have you heard someone say, "I don't get even, I get revenge." Even though this is usually said jokingly, people tend to behave as if they really believe it. I know of situations where family members have not talked to each other literally for years because someone got their feelings hurt or felt they were wronged in some way. How many marriages have been destroyed because the spouse would not let go of a hurt, but kept bringing the pain up over and over like a sharp knife, cutting the soul of their mate? How often have we seen church members feuding with each other and trying to get others to take sides, sometimes splitting up a church family over trivial issues like the color of the church carpet or the style of worship music? Are we not supposed to esteem others higher than ourselves and put our own selfish wants aside when it comes to sharing the gospel? I am not talking about compromising doctrinal issues where we have to stand firm on God's Word. There are certainly times when it is critically important to take a stand for what is Biblically right. I am talking about those things that are simply a matter of opinion, that have no biblical basis for being right or wrong, which grow and grow in our hearts until they spew out like a volcanic eruption, destroying everything in its path.

The concept of forgiveness is very misunderstood – sometimes because we try to make it too easy, but often because we try to make it too hard. Some people think that just not talking about a past hurt constitutes forgiveness. Others believe you need to truly forget about the incident that hurt you. Still others believe that the person responsible for causing them hurt must come and apologize and ask for forgiveness before being forgiven. I think some key questions must be answered to better understand forgiveness: What happens if we don't forgive? Are there consequences if we choose not to forgive someone? What does it mean if we do forgive someone? How do I forgive?

So what is forgiveness? Let me begin by stating what forgiveness *is not*. Forgiveness is not simply letting someone off the hook. By this, I am saying that forgiveness does not mean that the person who hurt you or committed a serious sin against you no longer has any consequences to face. If someone murdered your child, they should be tried and sentenced according to the law. You can forgive someone without removing the appropriate consequences. You may ask: "Well doesn't God remove the consequences from us when we are saved?" The answer is usually not, with regards to the here and now. For example, if someone lives a sinful lifestyle and contracts HIV/Aids, and then comes to a personal relationship with Jesus Christ, does God take away the HIV/Aids? Usually not! God certainly can miraculously heal, but He usually does not remove the consequences of sin.

Consider when King David committed adultery with Bathsheba. She became pregnant, and David ultimately killed her husband to try to cover his sin. Finally, when confronted, David confessed his sin before God and repented. Then God told him that the baby born from this adulterous relationship would die. David prayed and fasted for many days hoping God would spare the child. But then the baby died. Even though David had confessed and repented, he still suffered the consequences of his sin. So forgiveness is not simply letting someone off the hook.

Forgiveness does not mean that you leave yourself open to future sins by the person that hurt you. God does not call Christians to be doormats! This is an idea and a lifestyle that has become far too prevalent. You must take a stand against sin while at the same time you exercise grace and forgiveness towards the person who hurt you. If a woman was being beaten by her husband, she should remove herself from that situation and find a safe home in which to stay. She should forgive her husband for his behavior but not allow herself to continue to be hurt by him. And forgiving him does not mean that she should not take legal action against him in order to protect herself and her children.

Forgiveness is not forgetting. How many of us can really forget something that has caused us deep emotional pain and suffering? We are not like God. God says when we ask for forgiveness that He casts our sins as far as the east is from the west. He will hurl them into the depths of the sea, where He will no longer remember them. But as human beings, we are simply not made that way. We do not have the capacity to forget. So you can forget about forgetting!

Just as others have hurt us, there will be times when we will undoubtedly hurt others, whether intentional or not. When that occurs, we need to seek forgiveness for the harm we have done. Asking for forgiveness is not the same as saying "I'm sorry." That may surprise you. You may have always thought these were the same thing. But there is a very real difference between saying "I'm sorry!" and asking "Will you forgive me?" and it goes beyond semantics. This is really important. It is something you should teach your children, and it is something you need to remember as you approach the throne of God. So what is the difference? When you say "I'm sorry," you are making a statement that requires no response or reaction on the part of the person to whom you are saying it. In other words, you are in control, and they are not. You may even think that whether or not they accept your apology is up to them, that you have done all you need to do. The critical point is that **you are the one who is in control!**

Now let's compare that to the phrase: "Will you forgive me?" Who is in control here? It is the other person – the person from whom you are asking forgiveness. You have taken yourself out of the position of control and left yourself completely vulnerable to them. You have given them the choice of whether or not to forgive you, and you are at their mercy.

So let me ask you – which way do you approach God? Do you approach Him with you being the one in control, or do you approach Him as Lord God Almighty, with Him having all of the power, and with you being at His mercy? I believe we should always approach Him asking for forgiveness and seeking His mercy. We should specifically confess our sins and ask His forgiveness for each one that He brings to our minds.

So now that we know what forgiveness is not, let me try to define what forgiveness is. In the New Testament, there are three Greek words that were translated as "forgive." The first word is *aphiemi* which means to "let go." When we forgive someone, we are releasing them. We are not saying that a wrong done in the past is now right or that what happened does not matter. We are not "letting them off the hook." We are letting go; we are "turning loose our grip" on the matter. We will no longer hold onto the hurt or try to get even with that person for the harm they have caused us. We are making a choice to give the hurt, the pain, and any thoughts of revenge up to God. As Romans 12:19 says: *Do not take revenge, my friends, but leave room for God's wrath, for it is written: "It is mine to avenge; I will repay," says the Lord.*

An excellent example of where this word is used is in Matthew 6:9-15 at the end of the Lord's Prayer.

> *Our Father in heaven, hallowed be your name, your kingdom come, your will be done on earth as it is in heaven. Give us today our daily bread. Forgive [aphiemi] us our debts as we have forgiven [aphiemi] our debtors. And lead us not into temptation, but deliver us from the evil one. For if you forgive [aphiemi] men when they sin against you, your heavenly Father will also forgive [aphiemi] you. But if you do not forgive [aphiemi] men their sins, your Father will not forgive [aphiemi] your sins.*

What Jesus is saying here is that if you "let go" of the sins someone has committed against you, the Father will also let go of the sins you have committed against Him. But if you refuse to let go of the sin of others, then neither will the Father let go of the sins you have committed. Now that is strong language! I cannot fully explain how this fits with God's unlimited grace and forgiveness at salvation, but this passage is very plain and difficult to misinterpret.

The second word for forgiveness is very similar. It is the word *apoluo*. It means "to release" or "to set free." It is used in Luke 6:37.

> *Do not judge and you will not be judged. Do not condemn and you will not be condemned. Forgive [apoluo] and you will be forgiven [apoluo].*

Again, it is clear that for you and me to be forgiven, we must forgive those that have sinned against us or caused us hurt.

The third word for forgiveness is *charizomai*. It comes from the word *charis,* which means "grace." In Second Corinthians 2:10-11, we read:

> *If you forgive [charizomai] anyone, I also forgive him. And what I have forgiven [charizomai] – if there was anything to forgive [charizomai] – I have forgiven in the sight of Christ for your sake, in order that Satan might not outwit us. For we are not unaware of his schemes.*

Paul was writing to the Corinthians about a person who had apparently been disciplined from the church because of a serious offense, but he had genuinely repented since that time. Paul is telling the Corinthians that they should lovingly restore this individual – that they should show *grace [charis]* to him and forgive him just as Christ forgives us. Forgiveness goes hand in hand with grace. It is where we give something to someone that they do not

# Forgiveness

deserve, just as God has shown us His grace and forgiveness.

Forgiveness is more than a vague concept. It is a process. Many stories in the Bible illustrate the process of forgiveness, but one of my favorites is from the Book of Genesis. It is the story of Joseph. We need to start back before Joseph was born to get the whole story. It begins with his father, Jacob.

Jacob tricked his brother, Esau, and his father and received Esau's blessing and birthright. Then he became so afraid for his life that he left and ran away to his uncle Laban in Haran. There he met Rachel, Laban's younger daughter, and he fell in love with her. Jacob served Laban for seven years in order to have Rachel as his wife. But on his wedding night, he was tricked and was given Rachel's older sister Leah instead. After agreeing to work seven more years, Laban gave him Rachel as well. Now Leah had a female servant named Zilpah, and Rachel had a female servant named Bilhah.

Leah began to have children first, and she had six sons. Jacob also had two children each by Zilpah and Bilhah, but Rachel could not have any children. Then we read in Genesis 30:22

> *Then God remembered Rachel; he listened to her and opened her womb. She became pregnant and gave birth to a son and said, 'God has taken away my disgrace.' She named him Joseph, and said, 'May the Lord add to me another son.'" And the Lord did that as well by giving her Benjamin; but she died in childbirth.*

Remember, Jacob loved Rachel more than Leah. And he loved Joseph and Benjamin more than his other sons because they were born to Rachel. Of course, the other sons knew this. And one day, while they were out in the field, they saw Joseph coming and made a plan to kill him. But Rueben, the oldest, did not want to see his brother dead, so he convinced his brothers to throw Joseph into a well, planning to rescue him later. However, while Rueben was away, his other brothers sold Joseph into slavery. Joseph was taken to Egypt, and he was wrongly accused of sexual assault by Potiphar's wife. He was thrown into prison. But God was with Joseph and blessed him (Genesis 39:21).

May I chase another rabbit for just a minute? I wonder if you would feel blessed if you were in Joseph's situation. I have to admit that I do not believe I would. He was separated from his family, wrongly accused, and thrown in prison. And yet we read that the Lord was with him, and he continued to be faithful to the Lord in spite of his circumstances. So what is the point? It is essential that we not view God's love for us based on our circumstances at any point in our lives; sometimes (like with Joseph), our circumstances are not the result of personal choices, but rather are simply the result of the sinful world we live in or the evil others intend towards us. But even the bad things can be used by God to accomplish His plans and purposes as we allow Him to work in us and through us. We must keep in mind Romans 8:28

> *And we know that in all things God works for the good of those who love him, who have been called according to his purpose.*

Notice that God does not promise that we will like everything that happens to us, nor does He promise to protect us from bad things. What He says is that "in all things," He works for the good of those who love Him. This marries God's sovereignty into man's free will to choose. And even when others choose to do evil to us, God is still able to use those things (as we allow Him) to bring honor and glory to Himself.

Now back to Joseph, while he was in prison, he interprets a dream for the Pharaoh and is rewarded by being given the position of second highest in the land of Egypt. He foretells seven good years where the crops would be plentiful. But at the end of those seven years, a terrible famine would come. So the Egyptians stored up food during the seven good years, and when the hard years came, Joseph opened the storehouses to feed the people. (This was also an excellent example of patience, as we discussed earlier).

Even the land of Canaan where Joseph's family and all the Hebrews lived was hit by the famine, and Jacob sent his ten sons (Joseph's brothers) to Egypt. In Genesis 42:1-7, we read:

> *When Jacob learned that there was grain in Egypt, he said to his sons, "Why do you just keep looking at each other?" He continued, "I have heard that there is grain in Egypt. Go down there and buy some for us, so that we may live and not die." Then ten of Joseph's brothers went down to buy grain from Egypt. But Jacob did not send Benjamin, Joseph's brother, with the others, because he was afraid that harm might come to him. So Israel's sons were among those who went to buy grain, for the famine was in the land of Canaan also. Now Joseph was the governor of the land, the one who sold grain to all its people. So when Joseph's*

> *brothers arrived, they bowed down to him with their faces to the ground. As soon as Joseph saw his brothers, he recognized them, but he pretended to be a stranger and spoke harshly to them.*

Now think about this. It had been almost twenty years since Joseph had seen his family. Twenty years in a foreign land separated from his flesh and blood. Then his brothers show up. Here they are standing before him, and he does not even acknowledge that he knows them. In fact, it says that he spoke harshly to them. He basically calls them liars when they begin to tell him about their father and their younger brother. I can imagine that those feelings of anger might have welled up in him as his slavery and separation from his father came to his mind. He probably thought of the pain and suffering he had experienced – the time in the cold prison, the years in slavery, being sold by his own brothers. But then notice in Genesis 42:18-24, Joseph's heart began to soften.

> *On the third day, Joseph said to them, "Do this and you will live, for I fear God: If you are honest men, let one of your brothers stay here in prison, while the rest of you go and take grain back for your starving households. But you must bring your youngest brother to me, so that your words may be verified and that you may not die." This they proceeded to do. They said to one another, "Surely we are being punished because of our brother. We saw how distressed he was when he pleaded with us for his life, but we would not listen; that's why this*

*distress has come upon us." Reuben replied, "Didn't I tell you not to sin against the boy? But you wouldn't listen! Now we must give an accounting for his blood." They did not realize that Joseph could understand them, since he was using an interpreter. He turned away from them and began to weep, but then turned back and spoke to them again. He had Simeon taken from them and bound before their eyes. Joseph gave orders to fill their bags with grain, to put each man's silver back in his sack, and to give them provisions for their journey. After this was done for them, they loaded their grain on their donkeys and left.*

Joseph's heart had begun to soften; he had to turn away from his brothers and weep. But he was not yet ready to forgive them. He took his brother Simeon and had him bound in front of his other brothers. The Bible does not tell us how Joseph treated Simeon during the time his brothers were away. There is every indication that he was treated as a prisoner. It is apparent that Joseph did not reveal himself to Simeon during this time. So his own brother was with him for months, yet Joseph did not bring him into his home or treat him with kindness. Joseph's other brothers had returned to their father in the land of Canaan. They had enjoyed the food for a time, but then it ran out. When Jacob asked why they did not go back to Egypt to get more food, they told him they could not go back without taking his youngest son Benjamin. It was difficult for Jacob to let go of Benjamin, but eventually, he agreed, and the brothers headed back to Egypt along with Benjamin. When they arrived, Joseph told his steward to take them to his house. And we pick up the story in Genesis 43:26.

> When Joseph came home, they presented to him the gifts they had brought into the house, and they bowed down before him to the ground. He asked them how they were, and then he said, "How is your aged father you told me about? Is he still living?" They replied, "Your servant our father is still alive and well." And they bowed low to pay him honor. As he looked about and saw his brother Benjamin, his own mother's son, he asked, "Is this your youngest brother, the one you told me about?" And he said, "God be gracious to you, my son." Deeply moved at the sight of his brother, Joseph hurried out and looked for a place to weep. He went into his private room and wept there.

When Joseph sees his younger brother Benjamin, he has to run out of the room to find a place to weep. He was overwhelmed! He had finally been reunited with his own brother and his ten half-brothers. Only his father was missing from this family reunion. The emotion of seeing his true brother moved him deeply. The Bible says he wept. He did not just cry; he poured out his hurt, his full emotions of being separated from his family all those years. Finally, we read in Gen 45:1-2:

> "Then Joseph could no longer control himself before all his attendants and he cried out, "Have everyone leave my presence!" So there was no one with

*Joseph when he made himself known to his brothers. And he wept so loudly that the Egyptians heard him, and Pharaoh's household heard about it."*

All of this was part of the process of forgiveness – he had to recognize his past hurt and work through the bitterness and the pain from his years of loss, then finally make the choice to forgive his brothers for how they had so terribly mistreated him.

We have to do the same thing when we forgive. We have to let God bring to the surface those painful emotions we feel towards the person who hurt us. It has to touch us at the very core of our being, as it did Joseph. Then we must give up our right to hold that sin against the person who caused us harm. It is like writing that person's name on a helium balloon, then letting go of the string. We must let it go up to heaven and never reclaim that balloon again.

Forgiveness is not forgetting. You cannot forget about things people have done to hurt you deeply. Forgiveness is a choice – a decision of the will. It is not a feeling. It is something God requires us to do, whether we feel like it or not. Since God requires us to forgive, it is something we can do – something we must do! And we should not wait to forgive, hoping for the pain to go away. We should not wait until we feel like forgiving – we may never get there. Make the hard choice to forgive even though you do not feel like it. Once you choose to forgive, Christ can then begin to heal your hurts.

I love what Philip Yancey says in his book: *What's So Amazing About Grace*: "When we genuinely forgive, we set a prisoner free, and then we discover that the prisoner we set free was us."[1] You see, unforgiveness does far more to you – the one holding onto unforgiveness – than to the person you are unwilling to forgive.

To be quite honest, I was once a prisoner of unforgiveness. When my father passed away, my mother and I opened the home safe and took out a portfolio of important papers. We needed some of these to present to the mortuary, and we left the portfolio on our kitchen table while we went to the mortuary. My parents had taken care of my father's mother for several years. While my mother and I were at the funeral home, my father's sister came to stay with my grandmother. But while we were gone, she went through the files we left on the table and took out some important documents pertaining to my grandmother. She never bothered to ask; she just took them. Well, when I found out they were missing, I called her and gave her a piece of my mind – not that I had any to spare! I was furious. How could she have done such a thing on the day of my father's funeral? How could she have been so insensitive to the rest of the family?

So I promised myself I would have nothing to do with this lady ever again. She may have been my aunt, but there was simply no excuse for what she had done. That thought rolled over and over in my mind for the next two years. I still went to church. I still prayed and asked God to forgive my sins. But all the while, I was holding onto unforgiveness toward her. Then one day, I was reading the Parable of the Unmerciful Servant in Matthew 18.

> *Then Peter came to Jesus and asked, "Lord, how many times shall I forgive my brother when he sins against me? Up to seven times?" Jesus answered, "I tell you, not seven times, but seventy-seven times. "Therefore, the kingdom of heaven*

*is like a king who wanted to settle accounts with his servants. As he began the settlement, a man who owed him ten thousand talents was brought to him. Since he was not able to pay, the master ordered that he and his wife and his children and all that he had be sold to repay the debt.* "*The servant fell on his knees before him. 'Be patient with me,' he begged, 'and I will pay back everything.' The servant's master took pity on him, canceled the debt and let him go.* "*But when that servant went out, he found one of his fellow servants who owed him a hundred denarii. He grabbed him and began to choke him. 'Pay back what you owe me!' he demanded.* "*His fellow servant fell to his knees and begged him, 'Be patient with me, and I will pay you back.'* "*But he refused. Instead, he went off and had the man thrown into prison until he could pay the debt. When the other servants saw what had happened, they were greatly distressed and went and told their master everything that had happened.* "*Then the master called the servant in. 'You wicked servant,' he said, 'I canceled all that debt of yours because you begged me to. Shouldn't you have had mercy on your fellow servant just as I had on you?' In anger his master turned him over to the jailers to be tortured, until he should pay back all he owed.* "*This is how my heavenly Father will treat each of you unless you forgive your brother from your heart.*"

I saw that I had to forgive my aunt no matter how much she had hurt me. And that is the key. We have to recognize that the person who is really hurt by unforgiveness is the person holding onto it. It is like a cancerous tumor that continues to grow until we remove it. It makes people hard and bitter. Have you ever known someone who had grown old and hard and bitter? They probably had been hurt sometime in their life, and they became bitter as a result of holding on to unforgiveness. You might say: "You just don't know how much that person has hurt me!" And you are right; I do not know how deeply you have been hurt. If you could share with me every single detail of what that particular person did to you, I still would not be able to understand fully. But God does! God knows our hurts better than we know them ourselves. And the reality is that until you let go of your anger and unforgiveness, you are allowing that person to continue to hurt you. I once heard someone say that when you have to forgive someone more than God had to forgive you, you can stop forgiving. Think about that. How much did God have to forgive you?

Probably no one reading this has more to forgive than a lady named Cornelia. She was born on April 15, 1892. She was the youngest daughter of a Dutch watchmaker. She grew up and ran a Christian organization for girls in Holland until the German army invaded Holland in 1940. She and her family were arrested for hiding Jews in their home, and eventually, she and her sister Betsie ended up in a concentration camp called Ravensbruk.

While she was there, she witnessed terrible atrocities against the Jews. One day, her sister was beaten badly by a guard. But her sister encouraged Cornelia not to let any hatred come into her heart. She told Cornelia to forgive this man. Betsie constantly encouraged her younger sister to show God's love to others. But one day, Betsie became ill, and just a few days before Christmas in 1944, Betsie died. A week later, Cornelia was summoned to the guard station. She did not know what to expect. But to her surprise, they released her. They gave her small number of personal possessions back and sent her home to Holland. It was not until sometime later that she learned she had been released by mistake, and that the next month, all of the women her age in Ravensbruk were killed.

After she was released, Cornelia began to offer help to those who had suffered at the hands of the Germans. She set up a home where people could come for rehabilitation. And she began to speak at different places around the world. You may have already guessed who Cornelia was. She is better known as Corrie Ten Boom. Her whole family was killed during the war. In one of her speaking engagements, the guard who had been responsible for beating her sister came up to Corrie after her talk. She saw his face as she shook the hands of the people in front of him. And she wondered what she would do when he finally reached her. When his time came, this guard reached out his hand and asked Corrie to forgive him. And she said God broke through to her heart at that moment, and she was able to let go of her anger and truly forgive this man. Does this stir your spirit as much as it does mine? God used Corrie Ten Boom as a modern example to all of us of how much He loves us, and when we can really grasp that concept, we have to forgive others as we show God's love toward them.

And that forgiveness must be permanent. In Corrie Ten Boom's book *Tramp For The Lord* [2], she relates a story from later in her life. Listen to her words.

*I recall the time — and I was almost seventy — when some Christian friends whom I loved and trusted did something which hurt me. You would have thought that, having been able to forgive the guards in Ravensbruk, forgiving Christian friends would be child's play. It wasn't. For weeks I seethed inside. But at last I asked God again to work His miracle in me. And again it happened: first the cold-blooded decision, then the flood of joy and peace. I had forgiven my friends; I was restored to my Father.*

*Then, why was I suddenly awake in the middle of the night, rehashing the whole affair again? My friends! I thought. People I loved. If it had been strangers, I wouldn't have minded so.*

*I sat up and switched on the light. "Father, I thought it was all forgiven. Please help me do it." But the next night I woke up again. They'd talked so sweetly too! Never a hint of what they were planning. "Father!" I cried in alarm. "Help me!"*

*Then it was that another secret of forgiveness became evident. It is not enough to simply say, "I forgive you." I must also begin to live it out. And in my case, that meant acting as though their sins, like mine, were buried in the depth of the deepest sea....*

*Many years later, after I had passed my eightieth birthday, an American friend came to visit me in Holland. As we sat in my little apartment he asked me about those people from long ago who had taken advantage of me.*

*"It is nothing," I said a little smugly. "It is all forgiven."*

*"By you, yes," he said. "But what about them? Have they accepted your forgiveness?"*

*"They say there is nothing to forgive! They deny it ever happened. No matter what they say, though, I can prove they were wrong." I went eagerly to my desk. "See, I have it in black and white! I saved all their letters and I can show you where...."*

*"Corrie!" My friend slipped his arm through mine and gently closed the drawer. "Aren't you the one whose sins are at the bottom of the sea? Yet are the sins of your friends etched in black and white?"*

*For an astonishing moment I could not find my voice. "Lord Jesus," I whispered at last, "who takes all my sins away, forgive me for preserving all these years the evidence against others! Give me grace to burn all the blacks and whites as a sweet-smelling sacrifice to your glory."*

*I did not go to sleep that night until I had gone through my desk and pulled out those letters – curling now with age – and fed them all into my little coal burning grate. As the flames leaped and glowed, so did my heart. "Forgive us our trespasses," Jesus taught us to pray, "as we forgive those who trespass against*

> us." In the ashes of those letters I was seeing yet another facet of His mercy....
> Forgiveness is the key which unlocks the door of resentment and the handcuffs of hatred. It breaks the chains of bitterness and the shackles of selfishness. The forgiveness of Jesus not only takes away our sins, but makes them as if they had never been. Amen.

When we really forgive someone, it must be complete and permanent, because that is the way God forgives us. We cannot hold onto evidence that we can bring back out later to hold over the person who hurt us. That is not true forgiveness. That is just pretending to forgive, pretending there is no longer any issue. True forgiveness means letting it all go.

Finally, we must answer the question: "Who should we forgive?" Some people think that the person who hurt them must ask for forgiveness sincerely with a repentant heart (not just because they got caught) in order to be forgiven. Others believe we should not forgive anyone who continues to do the same things over and over – that we should withhold forgiveness until they change their ways. But I do not find anything at all like that in the Bible. We are commanded to forgive as God forgave us, and leave a person's sin between them and God. So who are we to forgive? We must forgive everyone, whether they ask for forgiveness or not.

While you are at it, make sure to include yourself in the list of those you are forgiving. Sometimes we are hardest on ourselves. We will not forgive ourselves for something God has long since forgiven us for. So let go of the hurt and unforgiveness you have toward yourself. Regardless of what you have done, if you ask Him, God forgives you. And if

He can forgive you, there is no reason not to forgive yourself.

The final person you need to forgive is God. This may surprise you because God could never sin against you. But you may have a hurt in your life that you blame God for. Something terrible may have happened to you, and you sometimes think, "Well, God could have prevented that from happening." And yes, God could prevent bad things from happening, but if He stopped every bad thing from happening, then there would be no choice. There would be no sin. The world would be perfect because no one could choose to do evil. There could be no murder, no rape, no hatred. That would be heaven. And it will be someday. But not here, and not now. For now, we have the freedom to choose, and some will choose evil. We may experience the consequences of their evil choices, but we must choose to forgive them so we are not held in the bondage of our own unforgiveness.

Right now, would you be willing to pray and ask God to reveal any unforgiveness in your own heart? Ask Him to begin to bring to your mind the names of anyone you are holding a grudge against. Maybe it's an old friend, perhaps a parent, perhaps a child. Whoever it is, remember it is you that is being held prisoner by your unforgiveness. Are you ready to begin the process of setting that prisoner free? Jot down the names of any persons God is bringing to your mind, and then spend some time in prayer, forgiving them and releasing them to God. I encourage you to take that step of letting go and letting God have that burden.

*F*ather God, I pray for the one holding a grudge, anyone who has realized that they are a prisoner of their own unforgiveness. Lord, I pray You would help them let go of that burden this very day. And as they confess the unforgiveness in their own heart, Lord, I pray You will heal their hurt and give them a new outlook on what You have in store for them as they shine Your light in this world.

In the book of Jeremiah, Your Word declares that You have plans for us; plans to prosper us and not to harm us; plans to give us hope and a future. Thank You for that promise of hope. Lord forgive us our sins. Make us whole again. I ask these things in Jesus' name. Amen.

## Questions to Ponder

1) Have you taken the time to seriously search your heart to see if any unforgiveness exists? If not, would you pray right now and ask God to reveal any grudges or unforgiveness you are harboring against anyone?

2) What would happen if you genuinely decided to forgive that person who hurt you very deeply? What would be the consequences or benefits of that decision?

3) Have you ever been hurt by God? Have things happened in your life that you blame God for? Are you willing to forgive God, even though He has not actually done anything wrong, so that you can be released from that unforgiveness? If yes, tell Him right now that you forgive Him.

4) Are you having a hard time forgiving yourself for something you have done in the past? What would happen if you chose to forgive yourself? What will happen if you continue without forgiving yourself?

5) Have you considered that there might be someone you have hurt deeply that you need to go to personally and ask them to forgive you? Could they be holding on to unforgiveness that is eating away at their life like cancer? Pray and ask God to help you know what He would have you do.

# Chapter 5

# Integrity

*"My goal in life is to be as good of a
person as my dog thinks that I am."*
Author Unknown

---

If there is one single description that I would like to have on my tombstone someday, it would read: "He was a man of integrity!" When you really think about it, what is the alternative? How would it make you feel if someone said: "He certainly is *not* a man of integrity!" Stop for just a moment and see if you can think of someone you would consider *not* to have integrity. How would you feel if you knew that was the way others thought of you?

I am deeply concerned that we have become a society in which true integrity is more and more rare. We begin by compromising our integrity in small ways that seemingly do not matter. Then as we become more accustomed to this, our conscience becomes hardened, and we begin to compromise our integrity in more significant ways.

Consider this hypothetical example. You and a friend decide to eat at a restaurant where you order a steak dinner with a side salad, and the person with you decides to eat from the "Megabar." You know the "Megabar" that has everything your heart desires, including unlimited salads, macaroni and cheese, vegetables, meats, fresh fruit, and a variety of desserts. If you live in the South, they usually have fried chicken and mashed potatoes with gravy. Suppose the person with you brought back a piece of pineapple or melon or strawberries or something that looked especially good, and you decided to take a taste. It was good, so you asked that person to get you a serving of that dish on their next visit to the "Megabar."

Some of you may be thinking, "What's the problem with that?" The problem is that you did not order from the "Megabar"; you ordered a steak from the menu with a side salad, and the Megabar was not included in the price of your steak and salad. Can I just be very frank with you; the reality is that you are *stealing!* You are taking something you did not pay for. At this point, you may think I am being absurd, that I am carrying things a little too far. You might say, "But it was just a few strawberries!" So let me ask you: Is that all your integrity is worth? Where do you draw the line when it comes to taking something for which you did not pay? Is it all right as long as it is worth less than a dollar or maybe ten dollars? If that is your definition, then it would be all right for your child to walk into a grocery store and pick up a piece of candy or a pack of gum and walk out with it. Is that right? Is that what you want your reputation to be? Is that what you want your family's reputation to be?

There is an old story about a man who propositioned a young lady by asking her if she would go to bed with him for a million dollars.

She quickly responded: "Well, yeah, for a million dollars."

To which the man replied: "Well, how about ten dollars."

The lady was infuriated and said: "What kind of lady do you think I am?"

The man answered: "We've already established that. Now we are just arguing over the price!"

You see, if you are willing to put a price on your integrity, you have already lost it.

When our twins were just toddlers, my wife would make her weekly trip to the grocery store and load them into a grocery cart. One day, she came home from the store and found one of our twins holding a thin green pepper he had picked up when she stopped in the produce area. She had no idea he was holding the pepper until they were home, but she immediately loaded the children back into their car seats and returned to the grocery store. She went with my son to the store manager, gave the pepper back, and made him apologize for taking it. Many of you might laugh at this story, but my wife was able to teach my twins a very important lesson that day. There are consequences for doing wrong. It caused them some embarrassment and an extra trip to the store. It required my son to confess his crime and to give back the stolen property. She could have thought it was only a small pepper, worth less than a dollar. Or she could have argued that the twins were too young, and it would not make any difference to them anyway. But the problem with that kind of thinking is that it requires you to be a certain age or have a specific dollar value assigned to an item before integrity matters. The message we need to communicate is that integrity matters all the time.

I work for a company with a written "Code of Conduct," which is essentially a policy that requires employees to maintain the highest levels of integrity. One of the things I like about it most is the statement that reads: "Our Code of Conduct is fully in effect...all the time...everywhere." This leaves no room for personal interpretation about conducting business in an unethical manner, but it also goes beyond that. It says that it matters all the time, regardless of where you are. Whether an employee of our company is on the job or not, it is recognized that they are connected with our company, and they represent our company and its values all the time. If someone has the reputation of being dishonest away from work, that reputation will carry over into the workplace. That character trait cannot be turned on and off at a whim. So our employees are expected to be people of integrity, which should extend to all facets of their lives. As Christians, God has given us a "Code of Conduct" – His Word! His "Code of Conduct" is in effect all the time, everywhere. Integrity should be the flag we fly as Christians following our Lord Jesus Christ.

Recently, I read about college students being prosecuted for downloading songs from the internet onto their computers or MP3 systems without paying the author for his work. Although many people do not think about this as stealing, that is precisely what it is. It seems that many people never give this a second thought. However, if they worked hard to purchase something which was stolen from them, they would be highly upset. Can you imagine how distressed a college student would be to have his laptop or car stolen (maybe not as disturbed as mom or dad who is paying for it!). Do you think the student would simply say: "Well, that's no big deal! I guess they needed it more than I did."

Some people would say that downloading a song is not stealing since you are not physically removing an item that the owner can miss. But it is stealing. You are stealing income from the author who created the song. The song is the author's property, and it is the only thing he has to sell. "Burning a CD" is robbing him of the reward he deserves for his time and his talents.

I know a family who lives in Asia. The wife works for a factory that is owned by the government. At the end of each month, this business looks at the amount of money the company has made and decides whether or not they have enough money to pay the employees. Did you get that? After the employee has worked for an entire month, they may or may not get paid for their work, depending on whether or not the company believes it has made enough money. The company is stealing from its employees. And in the same way, anyone who takes something that has value without paying for it is guilty of stealing. They have prevented the owner from receiving his rightful earnings for the work he has done.

The concept of integrity seems to be missing not only in the hearts and minds of our young adults; it is missing in people of all ages. Parents are not instilling it in their young children. How can we teach integrity to someone else if it is not a fundamental part of our own lives? How common is it for a co-worker to take something from work, even if it is just a pen? Or maybe they take extra breaks or long lunches without making up that time. Isn't that stealing time that belongs to the employer because they are being paid for work they did not do? The Bible tells us that everything we do should be done for the glory of God. We should work hard because, in reality, we are working for the Lord. Everything we do represents who we are as Christians, and our integrity should be above reproach.

I related the story earlier about one of my twins taking the pepper, and my wife taking the boys and the pepper back to the store. Do you think this might have had an influence on the store manager? Could he have asked himself what would make a busy young mom do this for such an insignificant thing as a pepper? Could there have been others who overheard what happened and thought about how important integrity was to my wife and perhaps reevaluated some of their own decisions? You might think that is silly, that it did not really mean anything to anyone else.

Have you ever heard the story about Abraham Lincoln, who walked over six miles to return a few pennies a woman had overpaid for merchandise? From this act, he was given the name "Honest Abe" because he wanted his integrity to be unquestionable. His integrity mattered to him, and his actions have undoubtedly influenced many thousands of individuals since that time.

What about integrity in our finances – in our giving to God? Some people think that because we live in the age of "grace," we are no longer under the "Old Testament Law," and therefore, we are not required to give 10% of our income to God. But the word tithe means 10%, and we are commanded to pay our tithe, and anything above that is a free-will offering. Tithes and offerings are two different things. A tithe is a debt you owe, and an offering is a gift you give. The Bible is clear that we are supposed to tithe and that failing to tithe is robbing God. In Malachi 3:8, it says:

> *"Will a man rob God? Yet you rob me. But you ask, 'How do we rob you?' In tithes and offerings. You are under a curse – the whole nation of you – because you are robbing me. Bring the whole tithe into the storehouse, that there may be food in my house." Test me in this, says the Lord Almighty, and see if I will not throw open the floodgates of heaven and pour out so much blessing that you will not have room enough for it."*

# Integrity

In the final analysis, integrity is about a lifestyle. It reflects an attitude of the heart that desires to do what is right, no matter what others are doing. It means that you will do the right thing regardless of whether anyone else is watching. It reflects a moral character based on our love for God and a desire to honor Him. We recognize God sees all we do, and we do not live lives of integrity because of fear of God's punishment, but because of our love relationship with Him. It is that relationship that we do not want to damage in any way.

Similarly, our relationship with our fellow man is based on mutual respect and trust. If you violate that trust, it may never be regained. It is hard to develop trust for someone who has stolen from you in the past. How would you feel if you came into a room and saw your best friend taking $20 out of your wallet, thinking you were not watching? What would happen to your relationship?

Integrity also means being honest even though there may be negative consequences. What if you forget to do something you had committed to do or just made a mistake? Then you decided to tell a "white lie" to make yourself look better. There are no "white lies"; all lying is in opposition to the character of integrity. My experience has been that people who tell one lie are likely to keep lying about other things. I have heard it said that a liar must have a good memory because he must keep telling new lies to cover up his previous ones. Is that the way you want to be characterized?

So from a very practical standpoint, how do we live a life of integrity? What does it look like? There was a popular saying a few years ago called "WWJD" – What Would Jesus Do? People wore bracelets with these initials to remind them that they should keep God's perspective in all circumstances of life. It may surprise you to find that this saying originated in a book written in the late 1800s by Charles M. Sheldon, entitled, *In His Steps —What Would Jesus Do?* [1] It is the story of a pastor who thought eloquent preaching was what his role was all about. Then one day, a stranger came to town looking for some work to earn money for food. Everyone in town turned him away, including the pastor. No one had time for him. After all, the pastor had important things to do, like preparing his sermon, which he had to deliver before his large congregation on Sunday. He could not be bothered with the needs of a stranger.

The stranger ends up dying after delivering a sober message to the congregation and the pastor about what he thought Jesus' words meant regarding helping the needy, feeding the poor, and giving shelter to the homeless. The words of the stranger, coupled with his sudden death, had a profound impact on the pastor, and he vowed to live his life differently – to live his life asking the question, "What would Jesus do?" when faced with different situations in life. Although the question seems quite simple, it can provide an excellent moral compass when facing a decision with which you are struggling. Simply ask yourself: "What would Jesus do?" Or ask yourself: "What would I do if Jesus were standing here beside me right now?" After all, if you are a Christian, He is with you all the time.

The Bible teaches that we should live our lives above reproach. That means that everything we do should be done in such a way that no one would ever have anything bad to say about us; no one would ever question whether we were doing the right thing or not.

Let me share a personal example. When my twins graduated from High School, some of their friends invited them to spend the night at their house.

At first, I had no problem; then, I found out it was a co-ed sleep-over. The parents were there, so there were chaperones. The girls and the guys were sleeping on separate ends of the house. But a house provides an intimate environment, and with a house full of teenagers, I knew two parents could not keep up with everyone all the time. I also knew this was a particular time of vulnerability in the lives of the graduates, because many would go off to college and never see each other again. It was a time filled with emotions, dreams, and wishes.

I told my kids that I would not make the decision for them, but I wanted them to know I disapproved of them participating in the co-ed sleepover, and I gave them the reason why. My reasoning was simple: I did not want them to be in a position where their integrity could be tempted or questioned as a result of that evening; I wanted them to have a reputation of being above reproach.

Can it be said of you that you are living a life above reproach? What do people say about you when you are not around? Do they say: "You can always trust him!" If not, I want to encourage you to make the decision today to become that person of integrity. Ask God to help you remove those things from your life that prevent you from being the person of integrity He has called you to be.

---

*Father God, I pray for the one who is reading this and who has realized that they are not living a life of integrity. Lord, I pray for forgiveness for this person, and I pray that You would challenge their heart right now to make a new commitment to You to live a life that is above reproach. Help each of us to develop a lifestyle that places You at the center of all that we do, and that brings us to the point often of asking, "What would Jesus do?" Lord, I ask for Your protection on each of our minds and hearts: cover us with Your umbrella of protection. Help us keep our eyes fixed on You. I ask these things in Jesus' name. Amen.*

## Questions to Ponder

1) How would your friends describe your integrity? How would God describe your integrity? Does your outward appearance and actions accurately reflect what is in your heart?

2) What hinders you from living a life of integrity right now?

3) What would happen if you truly decided to live a life of integrity from the heart – totally transparent no matter who was watching you? What do you think would be the consequences or benefits of that decision?

4) How would you feel if you found out that your best friend was very different in their behavior when you were not around, and that they acted in ways that did not represent a life of integrity? What would you say to that person? Are you able to take that advice for yourself?

5) Are there things in your past that have reflected a lack of integrity that you have never addressed? If so, would you take the time right now to talk with God about this and seek His forgiveness? Ask His direction regarding anything else you need to do to make things right from any past actions.

6) What specific steps will you take to ensure that you live a life of integrity from this point forward (e.g., establish an accountability relationship with regular discussions about how you are living)?

# Chapter 6

# Love

*"If I speak in the tongues of men and of angels, but have not love, I am only a resounding gong or a clanging cymbal. And though I have the gift of prophecy, and can fathom all mysteries and all knowledge, and though I have a faith that can move mountains, but have not love, I am nothing. If I give all I possess to feed the poor, and surrender my body to the flames, but have not love, I gain nothing. Love is patient; love is kind; it does not envy; it does not boast, it is not proud; it is not rude, it is not self seeking; it is not easily angered; it keeps no record of wrongs; love does not delight in evil, but rejoices with the truth; it always protects, always trusts, always hopes, always perseveres. Love never fails. But where there are prophecies, they will cease; where there are tongues, they will be stilled; where there is knowledge, it will pass away. For we know in part and we prophesy in part. But when perfection comes, the imperfect disappears. When I was a child, I talked like a child, I thought like a child, I reasoned like a child. When I became a man, I put childish ways behind me. Now we see but a poor reflection as in a mirror, then we shall see face to face. Now I know in part, then I shall know*

*fully even as I am fully known. And now these three remain: faith, hope, love. But the greatest of these is love."*
— *I Corinthians 13*

---

What can be more powerful than God's description of love! Before we go any further, let me ask you: Have you ever truly been loved? What was it like? How would you describe it? What did the other person do to let you know how much they really loved you? Did they tell you they loved you, or did they show you they loved you by their actions toward you? If I were to ask you to write down ten things that genuinely let you know you were being loved, what would you write down? Take a moment right now and see if you can make a short list. Write down your thoughts on a separate sheet of paper or in the margins of this book.

Turning that question around: "Have you ever truly loved someone else?" Did the person you loved know that you loved them? How did they know? Was it because you told them you loved them, or did you take some action that showed them that you truly loved them? Again, let me ask you to think about that person you genuinely loved and make a short list of how you think you let them know that you loved them. Write down your thoughts on a separate piece of paper or in the margins of this book.

When I asked if you had ever been loved, some of you may have had a knot in your stomach. Thinking about this question was emotionally painful. Some of you may have been physically or emotionally abused or suffered under a harsh parent. For others, you may associate the word "love" with some physical act that was pushed on you against your will, and the concept of true love is foreign to you. If this describes you, perhaps you need to reread Chapter Four on forgiveness. Some of you have honestly never thought about the true meaning of love, and this chapter may be the beginning of a journey to help you grow in both giving and receiving true love.

True love is a concept that I believe is often misunderstood in our post-modern society. Many people think of love as simply a feeling. Some live their lives by the mantra: "If it feels good, do it!" But I assure you that is not love. Sometimes the word love is used lackadaisically, as in "I just love your new outfit!" or "I love that car!" But that is not love.

Love is a profound word, expressing some of the deepest emotions of human beings. Different people have various ways in which they like to be loved, and in which they like to give love. In Gary Chapman's brilliant book *The Five Love Languages*, he submits that every human being has at least one primary way in which they desire to be loved and to show their love to others. He calls this their "primary love language," which can be classified into one of five basic descriptions: words of affirmation or encouragement, quality time, receiving gifts, acts of service, and physical touch and intimacy. He says: "Understanding the five love languages and learning to speak the primary love language of your spouse may radically affect his or her behavior. People behave differently when their emotional love tanks are full."[1]

The old adage of opposites attracting is certainly evident when you look at the love languages of most couples. For example, in my own family, my primary and secondary love languages are physical touch and intimacy, and acts of service, respectively.

My wife's primary and secondary love languages are quality time and words of affirmation or encouragement.

A typical scenario in the Wofford home could look like this. I come home from a hard day at work, having used up all my words in meetings and talking with others on the phone. I sit down on the couch, wanting just to rest for a few minutes, and my wife comes into the room and sits on the love-seat so she can look at me. Her biggest desire is for me to spend some quality time just talking with her and listening to her. She wants words of encouragement from me. But I am tired from the day and do not feel I have any words left to say. Besides, I just want to be cuddled and held, have my back rubbed, or have her fingers run through my hair as she loves me with "physical touch." Or, at the very least, I want her to be preparing my dinner or offer me something to drink as I relax for a minute on the couch – loving me with her "acts of service." But these are as foreign to her as me talking with her and sharing that "quality time" in her love language. In the end, neither of us feels loved because the other one is speaking in their primary love language and seeking to be loved in their primary love language. So through our twenty-six years of marriage, we have had to work at communicating in each other's love language. We had to set aside personal desires in order to show love in a meaningful way.

The same is true with our children. It is vital to understand how to say "I love you" to each child individually and not assume that what you do to make one feel loved will make another feel the same way – each one has his or her own unique way of feeling loved. When our kids were younger, one of our sons felt most loved when someone spoke "encouraging words" to him, and our youngest son felt most loved when he was "receiving a gift." It did not have to be anything significant; any gift would do. His favorite type of gift was little stuffed animals. In fact, he loved to sleep with all of his stuffed animals cuddled up in bed with him.

I remember a time when our children were young, and I asked them to clean their rooms. But when I came home from work, nothing had been done. (That may be hard for you to imagine, but it really happened in our home – actually more than once). I called the kids into our Family Room for "a discussion" and spoke to them sternly about their disobedience and my disappointment. One of my sons began to cry almost immediately. The other listened but did not react emotionally.

After our discussion, they immediately got to work cleaning up their rooms. I wanted to reward their positive response (even though it was the second time that I had asked!), so I stopped by the store the next day and bought each of them a little stuffed animal. My youngest son was ecstatic. Remember, he loved it when I would bring home little gifts (his primary love language is "receiving gifts," which means he feels especially loved when I would get him even the smallest present). My older son said thanks and tossed the stuffed animal on his bed. Then he went to talk with his mom about his day.

At the time, I did not understand why my older son was not more appreciative when I had gone out of my way to bring him a little reward. However, after learning about how each child is unique in the way they desire to be loved, it became clear that I was not talking in his primary love language. He would much rather I sit with him and encourage him with my words. He just wanted his daddy to let him know how proud he was of him, to show some interest in him by talking and listening to him. And I also realized that the reason he was so hurt when I scolded him for not cleaning his room the first time was that he was responding to my harsh words. You see, my "discouraging words" made him feel very unloved in the same way that my "encouraging words" made him feel loved. He was sensitive to my words, whether encouraging or discouraging, and I had to learn to be more careful when I spoke to him. So I encourage you to consider the love language of the one you want to show love to and give it in a most meaningful way to *them*.

If I could share only one piece of advice about how to show love to your wife and kids, it would be to spell love – T·I·M·E. As I shared in the first chapter on priorities, spending time with our families is the most critical way we, as husbands and fathers, communicate that we love them. This is putting the words "I love you" into action, and there simply is no substitute for time spent building relationships. And that is true in all love relationships – whether with our family, friends, or God. To demonstrate how much we really love them requires that we give an appropriate amount of time developing and nurturing that relationship.

One of my sons is engaged to be married. Can you imagine if he told his fiancée that he loved her, but he never spent any time with her? It would not take her long to realize that his words were empty and that he did not love her at all. The truth is that he cannot wait to spend time with her. When he is doing homework, he gets distracted as he thinks of her. He longs for the time when they are married so he can spend even more time with her. Men, I encourage you to do some introspection, and I challenge you to regain your focus on loving your wife and family, and to make them a priority again. Show them your L·O·V·E by giving them your T·I·M·E.

Another aspect of love in which few people succeed is loving others who are different from them. There is a man in our church named Marc, who is one of my heroes. He is a principal in an elementary school. Marc has a heart for underprivileged kids. He saw how great the needs were among a particular group of kids in his school, and he determined to do something about it. He invited others to join him in volunteering a Saturday morning once each month to go into low-income housing projects and spend some time just showing love to these kids. We played games, shared a Bible story, sang songs, had a craft project, and fed the kids a light snack. This effort grew until there were different groups of volunteers visiting several housing projects throughout the month. And I am certain for some of these kids, it was the first time they really understood what it meant to be loved. They were different than most of the people in our middle-class church. And it would have been easy just to ignore that they even existed or to say – "They don't look like me," or "They don't smell like me," or "They don't talk like me." But like Jesus who left the splendor of heaven to come to earth (which was filled with people who did not look like Him, smell like Him, or talk like Him) to be born in a stinky barn full of dirty animals – Marc saw human beings that God created who needed to know the love of a Savior. He was willing to be Jesus to them.

I remember one young boy in particular. He was probably five or six, but he loved to crawl up in my lap as Marc shared the Bible story. He would grab my hands and pull my arms around him like he was wrapping himself in a warm blanket. He listened intently as Marc shared how much Jesus loves us, and I think the young boy just wanted to feel that love. For some of these kids, Marc and his group of volunteers may be the only display of Jesus' love they will ever know.

---

English is a wonderful language, but it also has its shortcomings when trying to clearly define a complicated word like "love." If we could travel back in time to the Greek civilization, we might better understand some key concepts to this important word. In fact, some of our modern English words are grounded in their Greek roots. The ancient Greek language actually had many words which we sometimes translate as love, including: "eros," "thelo" (from the noun "thelema"), "phileo," and "agape."

The first word, "eros," is a word that connotes sexual love. In Greek mythology, the god of Eros was the god of "love" – or more precisely, the god of lust. He was worshipped as a fertility god. We get the English word "erotic" from this Greek root.

The second word, "thelo," is a verb that could be translated "to like." It would be the word used when we say "I love your new car" or "I loved that dessert you prepared last week." Obviously, we do not actually *love* an inanimate thing like a car or dessert, but using this word expresses an exaggerated feeling or desire we have about these things.

The third Greek word for love is "phileo," which means "brotherly love" and is the basis for several English words, including: Philadelphia – the city of brotherly love; and philanthropy – caring for humanity. It is a conditional love rooted in the emotions of men and women. It can be destroyed by jealously, hurtful words, anger, and many other sins of the heart. It is not the pure unconditional love of the next word, "agape."

"Agape" describes the unconditional, God-like love – a love not based on anything anyone else does or does not do; it is not dependent on a response. It describes the kind of love that should exist between a husband and wife – a love for each other not based on performance or behavior, not based on how either one feels or what they do, but a love based on uncompromising commitment. It is a love that never fails. It is a love that is "in spite of" rather than "because of." Sadly, this type of love is rare in post-modern America. The love expressed in a wedding vow "till death do us part" is often fleeting words rather than a genuine commitment of agape love. But we can be sure that God loves us with this type of love. Romans 5:6-8 says:

> *"You see, at just the right time, when we were still powerless, Christ died for the ungodly. Very rarely will anyone die for a righteous man, though for a good man someone might possibly dare to die. But God demonstrates his own love for us in this: while we were still sinners, Christ died for us."*

Did you know God loved you that much? Who else do you know who would die for you? Who would make this unbelievable sacrifice? Christ willingly died for us and expressed that unconditional love toward us. He loved us even while we were still sinners. He loved us before we were even born. And He still loves every person in that same way today. That does not mean He is not a righteous God who will judge sin. He is able to love the sinner yet hate sin. But His heart desires to see every human being repent of their sinfulness, and accept the free gift of salvation that He offers to all. Second Peter 3:9 says: *"The Lord is not slow in keeping his promise as some understand slowness. He is patient with you, not wanting anyone to perish, but everyone to come to repentance."* It is only when we reject that free gift that we choose to live a life separated from God for all eternity.

I would like to close this chapter with a poem I wrote in 2002.

### Sounds Like Greek to Me!

Love is such a simple but complicated word,
Some may think this sounds totally absurd.
Ancient Greeks had four words to describe this, though:
Agape, phileo, eros, and thelo.

Agape is the unfailing love God adorns;
He loved us even before we were born.
This is a love that knows no end;
It is too great to fully comprehend.

Phileo is the love you have for a brother,
The family-type of love you have for another.
Philadelphia is the city of "Brotherly Love,"
This is one way we should show our love.

Eros is the passionate love of two lovers;
The intimate, amorous love under-the-covers.
The fireworks, the music, the eyes locked in stare,
Ignoring surroundings, without a single care.

# Love

Thelo is a word that means to "like."
"I love your new haircut"; "I love your new bike."
This is a loose translation of love,
Compared to the three words mentioned above.

So where does this leave us as we finish this work?
Are we any closer to finding love's quirks?
Love your neighbor and give from your heart,
If you give it all away, you'll have more than at the start.

---

*F*ather God, I pray for the one who is reading this, that they would know Your great love right now. Perhaps they have never really known what true love is. Lord, would You wrap Your loving arms around them so that they may know how much You do love them. And I pray for the person struggling to show true love to others – whether it is their wife, kids, parents, or people they work with. Lord, I pray that You would bring peace to troubled hearts; plant Your love in place of the turmoil, water it and make it grow into something beautiful as only You can.

    Lord, for the husband who is struggling to show love to his wife, I pray that You would intervene. Even though his wife may not offer him any love, I pray You would show him that You have commanded him to love his wife even as You have loved the church, and that "not loving her" is not an option.

*Lord, I pray You would help us to show love to those who are different than we are, just as You left Your home in heaven to come to earth to show us Your great love. Help us to put feet on our love – to go into the world to those who are hurting, those in need, and share with them out of the blessings You have given us. You genuinely bless us each day, and I thank You for demonstrating Your love to us.*

*It is so easy to tell You we love you, and yet our actions often indicate otherwise. We get so busy that we fail to spend time with You. Forgive us our sins and help us to be careful with our thoughts, our words, and our actions each day. Help us to learn how to love You.*

*I ask these things in Jesus' name.*
*Amen.*

## Questions to Ponder

1) How would you describe true love? Can you think of a time when you felt an overwhelming love from someone else? Specifically, what did they say or do that made you feel loved? List ten things that genuinely let you know when you are being loved.

2) What has been your most extraordinary outpouring of love towards someone else? What did you say or do that showed your love?

3) Do you believe that God loves you? Why? (Don't allow yourself to settle for a pat answer or one you may have heard in church. Think about this and see if you can identify specific ways God has demonstrated His love toward you).

4) Is there someone to whom you need to show your love? What specific steps will you take to ensure they know that you genuinely love them and that you are not simply saying empty words? List some specific steps now, along with a date on which you commit to complete each step.

a.

b.

c.

d.

## Chapter 7

# Accountability

*"We must reject the idea that every time a law's broken, society is guilty rather than the lawbreaker. It is time to restore the American precept that each individual is accountable for his actions."*
*- Ronald Reagan*

---

Accountability is a word people like to use when it applies to other people, but not when considering the action of one's own self. It brings with it the notion of responsibility and consequences for choices. It means taking ownership of our own foolish mistakes rather than trying to blame someone else. Some people think it is all right to blame someone else for their own poor decisions, and try to take advantage for personal financial gain. For example, a person actually sued a fast-food restaurant after they ordered a cup of coffee, placed it between their legs while driving, had to stop suddenly, and spilled hot coffee in their lap. They saw this as the restaurant's fault for serving hot coffee, and they took no ownership for their own action – they did not hold themselves to any level of accountability. Does this seem crazy and ridiculous to anyone else?

The truth is we are all accountable. I would suggest that each of us is accountable to four major entities: God, our families, our work, and others. And in fact, this is the order in which we are accountable, with our primary accountability being to God first, then to our families, then to work, and then to others. We will explore each of these accountabilities one by one and provide some examples and practical advice on how to hold ourselves to a higher standard.

First, we are all accountable to God. If you do not believe you are accountable to Him in this life, you will undoubtedly find the truth of this in the life to come. In Paul's letter to the Philippians, he writes:

> *Therefore God exalted him [Jesus] to the highest place and gave him a name that is above every name, that at the name of Jesus every knee should bow, in heaven and on earth, and under the earth, and every tongue confess that Jesus Christ is Lord, to the glory of God the Father.*
> *- Philippians 2:9-11*

Jesus is Lord of all creation. He was there when the earth was created, and the first chapter of John tells us that everything was created by Him. At the end of time, everyone will be judged by Him, based on whether or not they have a personal relationship with Him (which is the criteria for eternal life with Him), and to determine what level of rewards they will receive based on their obedience after they became a Christian.

One critically important point to make here is that being accountable to God and making Him the first priority in your life is not the same as making church your highest priority or accountability. These two are very different. Being accountable to a church, a local body of believers made up of people just like you and me, fits in the last category of being accountable to others, not in the first category of being accountable to God. God is perfect; churches (people) are not. Some people will not go to church because they believe it is full of nothing but hypocrites who say one thing but act the opposite. They expect the church to be perfect, and they totally miss the point of being in a community of believers where each one can exercise his or her gifts and complete the body. They not only miss the opportunity to bless others with their gifts from God, but they also miss being blessed by others using their gifts.

God always wants what is best for us; churches can be made up of selfish people who want only what is best for themselves. In being accountable to God, it is essential to remember that doing things *for* Him is not the same as spending time *with* Him, and God would rather have you spending time with Him than doing any job in the church you may be asked to do. Please understand that I am not suggesting that you do nothing to serve your church; on the contrary, the Bible requires us to use our spiritual gifts in order to complete the church. This requires the right heart attitude in order to please God. But it does not mean you should feel so compelled to take on every task you are asked to do in the church, with the end result being that you miss the mark of what God has called you to do. God does not want you to let *doing things* interfere with *spending time with* Him.

Think about it this way: do you think your wife would rather you clean the whole house and yard every day or spend time talking with her, listening to her needs, and developing a more intimate relationship with her? Although your spouse expects you to do the necessary work around the house, spending time with her must be a second priority. Likewise, God wants you to make Him your first priority. He wants you to spend time with Him. He wants you to get to know Him better; He wants you to have a close, personal relationship with Him.

In doing this, you will want to please Him, and you will be glad to be accountable to Him. This accountability is not a burden, but rather a safeguard to keep you from doing things that would destroy your life. Being accountable to God will keep you from cheating on your expense report at work, which could ultimately cost you your job when you are found out. Being accountable to God will keep you from being drawn into that relationship with another woman, tearing your marriage apart. Having that close relationship with God will help you respond in the right way when your children are disobedient. Understanding that our first accountability is to God is key to all of our other relationships. Most importantly, being accountable to God will keep you in close fellowship with Him. It will keep you in a place of fulfillment and meaning that can be found nowhere else.

Second to God, we are accountable to our families. Our wives and children depend on us to make wise decisions. They rely on us to bring home money from our jobs to provide food, shelter, and clothing. They depend on us to lead in making a decision on which neighborhood to live in and which church to attend. Our wives and children need us so much more than simply providing for their physical and financial needs; they need us to provide for them emotionally and spiritually. They depend on us to be there when they are hurting. There will be days when your wife or child has a bad day, and they just need you to wrap your arms around them and hold them. So what happens when a man chooses not to be accountable to his family? His family goes with unmet needs.

I know a man named Peter who has struggled for many years with holding a steady job. He is not lazy or untalented. He does not have a low IQ. In fact, he has a degree in Engineering. His biggest problem is that he struggles with self-worth and depression. And his family struggles even more. His wife has felt the weight of all the kids' needs – clothing, school supplies, house payments, groceries, helping with homework – and all the other things required of parents in raising a family. The kids are good kids, but they struggle with their self-image and even more with not having a dad around when they need him most. I spent time trying to help the dad. We had prayer breakfast together as frequently as he would accept my invitation. I tried to help him see himself differently – from God's perspective of worth. But he could not get beyond his own worthlessness.

Let me chase another rabbit trail for a minute for the person reading this who is struggling with self-worth. When we think about what something is worth – what its actual value is – this can be measured by what someone is willing to pay for it. For example, when selling a house, would you agree that the worth of that house is what someone else is willing to pay for it? Now think about that in light of what God the Father was willing to pay for you. God was willing to pay the life of His only Son Jesus for you and for me. That is what you are worth to God; that is how much He values you, how much He loves you. Let that sink in for a minute. Have you ever considered that you are worth that much to anyone? God loves you immensely. Do not let John 3:16-17 become stale.

*"For God so loved the world that he gave his one and only Son, that whoever believes in him shall not perish, but have eternal life. For God did not send his Son*

*into the world to condemn the world, but to save the world through him."*

With that in mind, the next time you begin to think about how worthless you are or how no one seems to love you, remember how much God loves you and the price He paid for you.

My friend Peter could never quite grasp how valuable he was in God's eyes. And that self-worthlessness played out in his actions. When he would lose a job, he would go into a self-deprecating mode and not shave or bathe for days or weeks. He camped out in the basement of his home and did not have meals with his family. The relationship with his wife had long disappeared, although she remained faithful to him. This man needed an accountability partner – someone who could look him square in the eye and tell him to stop feeling sorry for himself, to stop beating himself up, to get up and get going, to provide for his family. I would have gladly played that role, but he could not get beyond his belief in his own worthlessness, and he would not open himself up to that level of accountability.

Our third accountability is to our employers. It seems that many people feel no accountability for their actions when it comes to their jobs. They treat their jobs much differently than they would if they were self-employed.

I was recently part of a team interviewing college seniors for open positions within our company. One candidate, Jacob, had spent the previous summer in Denmark taking a summer lab. Jacob was brilliant and already had several job offers. He interviewed well, had a lot of confidence, and the interview panel concluded that we should offer him a job. There was a post-interview dinner that evening with all of the candidates. It was an informal gathering with other employees invited to interact with the students. During the dinner conversation, Jacob told one of our employees that he had learned how to save money when he was in Denmark. He found that he could use one train ticket and simply erase the dates each day and write in the next day. When our team learned about this, he was immediately taken out of consideration. Jacob had shown his true character, and we knew he would likely act in a similar way if we hired him. We had no desire to hire someone who would have no shame with stealing and even boast about it openly as if that were something to be proud of.

This episode made me wonder: how many employees take advantage of their employers, perhaps in more subtle ways? For example, in planning a business trip, how many employees would stay at a much nicer hotel than they would stay if it were their personal expense, or eat in high-priced restaurants paying for expensive wine or other alcohol, or take other excursions using company funds? Shouldn't we treat our employers the same as we would want to be treated if we were the employer? What if everyone who had a job treated their employer as if they were working for themselves and spent the company's money just as if it were their own money? Companies would be much more profitable, and employees would ultimately benefit because there would be no need for jobs to move to lower-cost countries. Companies could afford to pay the employees more or provide better benefits.

And most importantly, the employee would benefit in ways he or she could not imagine because he or she was honoring God. John the Apostle wrote in First John 5:3: "This is love for God: to obey his commands." God rewards our obedience, even though we may often fail to give him credit for the blessings we receive. God expects us to work hard and work for our employers as if we are working for God. And when we do that, God will honor us and our work, and He will bless us.

Finally, our fourth accountability is to others. Last winter, my wife joined a First Place group. This is a program designed for ladies focused on weight loss and spiritual growth. Before joining this group, my wife knew what she needed to do to lose weight — cut back on the calories she was consuming and get some exercise to burn more calories. However, she could not maintain the discipline needed to achieve her goal without someone to whom she could be accountable. And if we are honest, we are all like that in certain areas of our lives.

My personal struggle is that I have a sweet tooth. My wife makes the best chocolate chip cookies in the world. (All three of my sons just said "Amen!") In fact, when my youngest son takes a few of these cookies to school in his lunch bag, his classmates will begin bartering for them, offering something in exchange that they brought for lunch. And when she gets a warm batch out of the oven, I could get a tall glass of milk and eat two-dozen in one sitting. However, my loving wife has a way of holding me accountable, making sure I recognize that she did not bake four dozen cookies for my sole consumption. And of course, she is also thinking about my health and my weight!

I want to ask you to do something that you may think is foolish, but bear with me. I want you to find a mirror in your home where you can get a good look at yourself. Make sure it is located in a room where you can close yourself off so that no one else can see you or hear you. Now I want you to look yourself right in the eye and ask yourself these questions:

- What am I doing that would bring my family or me great embarrassment if it were published on the front page of tomorrow's newspaper?
- What is the deepest, darkest secret in my heart that I do not want anyone else to know?
- What is my greatest struggle right now?
- What is it that I need to confess, but I could never bring myself to tell anyone else?

Now go to that mirror and look yourself squarely in the eye and talk with yourself about each of these questions. Talk with that person in the mirror just as if they were your closest friend. Talk out loud and share those deepest secrets, knowing this person will never betray you by telling your secrets. Stop reading right now and do this.

Now that you have verbalized your deepest secrets, I want you to realize two things. First, God heard your words. He heard you describing your deepest hurts and your greatest struggles. But He already knew them anyway, so you did not surprise Him. The second thing I want you to realize is that person in the mirror will not hold you accountable for continuing in sin. He will not come to you when you are struggling with looking at pornography and ask you if you have been clean this week. He will not ask you whether or not you are drinking or doing drugs. He will not ask you if you are cheating on your wife. But you need to find someone that will hold you accountable. You need to find someone you can trust, someone with whom you can share your deepest struggles and not be condemned and not worry that they will share your secrets with anyone else. That person will become your accountability partner. And likewise, you will become his accountability partner. You will ask him the tough questions about how he lives his life, and you will help him when he struggles.

Now, this is really important. Being an accountability partner does not mean you condemn the person sharing his struggles; it means you recognize that he has struggles different than your own, that we each have them, and that this is a way of getting someone else to help us with our struggles while we, in turn, help them with theirs. And it is absolutely critical that you do not share his struggles with anyone else – not your wife, not your secretary, not your golfing buddy – not anyone. Unless he can be absolutely sure that he can be one hundred percent honest without fear of it ever getting out into the open, he will not be completely honest with you – and you will not be totally honest with him. So developing this level of trust with each other is absolutely essential to accountability.

In the book *Point Man*[1], Steve Farrar lists seven key questions that accountability partners should ask each other every time they meet. Knowing that you are going to be asked these questions helps to keep you accountable each day. The seven questions are:

1. *Have you been with a woman this week in such a way that was inappropriate or could have looked to others that you were using poor judgment?*
2. *Have you been completely above reproach in all your financial dealings this week?*
3. *Have you exposed yourself to any explicit material this week?*

4. *Have you spent daily time in prayer and in the Scriptures this week?*
5. *Have you fulfilled the mandate of your calling this week?*
6. *Have you taken time off to be with your family this week?*
7. *Have you just lied to me?*

I encourage you to find that person with whom you can begin to develop that accountability relationship. It should be clear that this accountability partner needs to be of the same sex – male to male, and female to female. You may think there is no way to find someone you could be this open with, but I assure you someone else would love to have you as an accountability partner.

An excellent place to look is in your church, perhaps your Sunday School class. Find someone who is like-minded and initiate a conversation. Ask if they have ever thought about having someone who will hold them accountable and see if they would be willing to play that role for you. Take it slow. Do not spill all your marbles in your first meeting. You do not want to overwhelm your accountability partner, and you want to be sure you can fully trust him. Begin with small things. Then wait and see how he responds.

I have had the privilege of having several accountability partners in my life. I will mention two specifically: Nelson and Ken. Nelson was a godly man who was careful in what he said and what he did. I developed a sense of trust with him that I could share anything. He was an excellent accountability partner who challenged me and encouraged me. I know I could still call him at any hour and share anything; he would listen and give me good advice.

Ken, however, was not as solid. He was in a position where he should have been completely trustworthy. I should have been able to talk with him freely about anything. However, as our relationship developed, I realized that Ken talked about other people and their problems too freely. He openly shared things about others that should not have been shared. He may have done so because he trusted me so much, but it left me with enough concerns that I could never be fully transparent.

I continued this relationship for some time because I felt he could help me in the areas in which I chose to share, and I also continued because I thought I could help him. He had a highly stressful job, and I could serve as a sounding board. But over time, that relationship drifted, and we began to meet less and less frequently. I share this to emphasize the importance of wisely choosing your accountability partner. Take it slow so that you can gain confidence that he is completely trustworthy and that he is willing to meet often enough so that it meets your needs and his needs.

Each of us is accountable to four entities: God, our wife and family, our employer, and others. If you treat these relationships with the proper care, keeping them in perspective and in the right order of priority, it will save you from much hurt and disappointment in the future.

---

# Accountability

*Father God, I pray for that man who is struggling with sin in his life, the person who desperately needs someone to whom he can be accountable. Lord, we know that we are accountable to You, and that when we do not deal with sin in our lives, it leads to destruction. Your Word tells us in James 1:14 that "each one is tempted when, by his own evil desire, he is dragged away and enticed. Then after desire has conceived, it gives birth to sin, and sin, when it is full-grown, gives birth to death." Father, we confess our sin before You right now, and we ask You to reveal every specific sin that needs to be confessed. We pray that You would give us the wisdom to choose an accountability partner that we can trust, a partner that we can share our most intimate secrets with and with whom they can do likewise with us. Help us to be faithful in our walk with You. Teach us and grow us in our knowledge of You and Your Word. Give us the discipline that we need to study, learn, listen, and walk the walk. Thank You for Your extraordinary love. Amen.*

## Questions to Ponder

1) Do you have an accountability partner? If not, who can you identify that you would trust with anything you might need to share? Make a short list of potential candidates and begin to pray about this.

2) What are you doing that, if it were published on the front page of tomorrow's newspaper, would bring you or your family great embarrassment?

3) What is the deepest, darkest secret in your heart that you do not want anyone else to know about? What is it that you wish you could confess, but you could never bring yourself to ever tell anyone else? Let me suggest that you write this down on a separate sheet of paper, then pray and confess it to God. After you have finished confessing this, take the paper and burn it. Use this as a reminder that you no longer have to worry about that secret. God has forgotten it, and you need to put it behind you as well. Mark it down here with a date and some way to remember that you gave this sin to God, and the devil can no longer condemn you with it.

4) What is your greatest struggle right now? What specific actions can you take to eliminate this struggle? Do you think having an accountability partner would help you with this struggle?

# Chapter 8

# Leadership

*"You are not here merely to make a living. You are here in order to enable the world to live more amply, with greater vision, with a finer spirit of hope and achievement. You are here to enrich the world, and you impoverish yourself if you forget the errand."*
  - *Woodrow Wilson*[1]

---

Some people believe that leaders are born that way. Others think that developing leadership skills takes special training, such as being in the military or being a CEO of a business. A friend of mine, Michael, shared some wisdom his grandfather gave him as a young boy. The grandfather said: "Son, there are three things you can do about any problem you have in life. You can complain about it, hoping that someone will hear you complaining and fix the problem. You can hold it inside, not letting anyone know anything is bothering you until the pressure builds up over days and weeks, and you finally explode, lashing out at someone who may not have had anything to do with the original problem. Or you can roll up your sleeves and work hard to try to make things better." I think this wise grandfather was describing authentic leadership – being actively involved in tackling problems rather than just complaining or stewing about them.

When you think of great leaders, what names come to mind? Perhaps it is a former President of the United States like George Washington or Abraham Lincoln. Maybe you think of a former school teacher or coach who modeled leadership qualities for you. Or perhaps it was a relative or someone close to you. For me, there are two prominent leaders that impacted my life: John Prince Wofford, my father, and Merrill D. "Peanut" Turner, my first boss. Neither of these men was well-known. Neither was a public speaker or author. In fact, neither man was well-educated; my father dropped out of school in the ninth grade, and Mr. Turner never earned his high school diploma. So you might wonder why I would consider these two men great leaders. Let me share a few stories that might provide some answers.

As I mentioned in the first chapter, my father worked hard in a cast iron foundry making sand molds for forty years. He did not have a high-paying job or a position of leadership at his work. He was not a Sunday School teacher. In fact, I can only remember one time when he tried to teach a Sunday School lesson, and it lasted only five minutes. Daddy had worked hard studying the lesson and preparing himself; he was just not a public speaker and could not find words to say to help drive home the message he wanted to communicate.

In spite of this, I learned from the unique leadership qualities that my father possessed. The first quality is that *he gave of himself to help others*. We lived in a neighborhood of older people, and it was not unusual for something to be broken like a leaky faucet or a bathtub drain. My father would take my brother and me to help, and we learned a lot about doing repairs around the house. We would do everything from plumbing to electrical, from working on a furnace to fixing a car. My father often described himself as a "jack of all trades and a master at none." We were not always successful, but he was not afraid to try to help someone. So the first leadership lesson I learned from him was to give of myself to help others in need.

The second thing about my dad was that *he was serious about God*. From the time I can first remember until I was a young teenager, we gathered together every evening as a family and read a chapter in the Bible. Then we prayed together, each one taking turns to say a prayer out loud. My father was also faithful to take us to church as often as the doors were open. So the second leadership quality I learned from him was to make God a priority in my life.

If I could summarize the leadership lessons I learned from my father, it would be that he taught me how to live my life obeying the greatest and second greatest commandments. As I shared in Chapter Three, these two commandments teach us to "love God" and "love others." Daddy taught me what that really looks like in life. It is easy to say we love God and that we love others, but to truly live our lives where we demonstrate that love is another matter. Although there were many other wonderful lessons I learned from my father, I will save them for the next book: *FATHERLY ADVICE ~ GROWING WISER.*

The second man that provided strong examples of leadership for me was Mr. Turner. He was the sole proprietor of Turner's Variety Store in Spartanburg, South Carolina. It was an old-fashioned General Store that sold everything from plow parts to kerosene lamps, from horse-shoes to candy, from molasses gates (most of you have no idea what a molasses gate is) to rare coins. People would come from all over to buy unique items. But most of Mr. Turner's customers were the local poor.

I began working for Mr. Turner when I was fourteen. My first assignment was to sort plow parts in the basement which had been dumped in a large pile. It took me three weeks to sort through these parts. It was some of the hardest and dirtiest work I had ever done. The year was 1973, and the pay was only $1.50 per hour. After three long weeks, Mr. Turner brought me upstairs and began training me as a sales clerk. I learned to do every job in the store, from cleaning toilets to taking inventory, from stocking soft drinks in the machine to balancing the books at the end of the day. I learned how to change wicks in kerosene heaters and repaired broken handles in shovels and hoes. I worked for Mr. Turner for seven years until he passed away during my early years in college, and I continued to work for his son until I finished college and began my career as a Chemical Engineer.

So what made Mr. Turner such a great leader? First, *he challenged me.* He never asked me to do something that I was incapable of doing, but he provided me with opportunities to learn and grow in areas outside my comfort zone. He knew I had mechanical skills, and when someone brought in a malfunctioning heater, he would allow me to see what was wrong. He often did not know himself how to fix the problem, but he encouraged me to study the issue and see if I could understand it. And I learned it was okay to fail. It was not the end of the world if I could not repair something that was already broken.

I remember one man who brought in an old pocket watch that was not working. My grandfather had been a watchmaker, and I knew a little about watches. I had cleaned and oiled a watch for this man before, but this one was in poor condition with a lot of rust. I tried to clean it, but it was beyond my ability to do anything with it. And that was okay. Mr. Turner never expected me to fix every problem that came through his door. In fact, as I look back, I believe this may have been an important lesson he wanted me to learn as well – I cannot always fix things. This was a hard lesson for me to learn in life because I was – I still am – a fixer. This became increasingly important later in my life as I had to deal with the fact that I could not fix things in the lives of my wife or children.

This leads me to the second point about Mr. Turner's leadership: he was a teacher, and *he taught me* many valuable things. One of the first practical things he taught me was how to count change when I sold something. He showed me that I should start with the sales amount, say $13.21, and the amount of money the customer gave me, say $20.00. I would open the cash drawer and take four pennies counting up as I took each one (22, 23, 24, 25 cents), then three quarters (50 cents, 75 cents, $14), then a dollar ($15), then a five-dollar bill reaching twenty dollars. I had never heard that before. Granted, this was before the days of calculators or sophisticated cash registers that calculate the change needed. Still, it was a great learning experience in how to count change for a customer. And it is a technique I still use today.

Mr. Turner taught me so much more. He not only taught me practical lessons; he taught me to have confidence in myself, to be fair and straightforward when dealing with others, and most importantly, to do what I promise to do.

The third aspect of leadership I learned from Mr. Turner was trust. *He trusted me.* Can I ask you a simple question: do people trust you? How much do they trust you? Do they trust you with everything they have? Mr. Turner trusted me that much. During the decade of the 1970s, there was a gold and silver rush. The price of gold and silver rose quickly to all-time highs. Mr. Turner had a coin shop in one corner of the store that his son, Virgil, started. Virgil bought and sold coins as well as bulk silver and gold. On more than one occasion, Virgil needed a large amount of cash to pay for a collection of coins. He sent me to the bank to bring back $20,000 or more in cash. How many people would have trusted a young teenager with such a large sum of money? There were other times when I was the only one in the store with full access to all the money in the cash drawer and in the safe. It was apparent that Mr. Turner trusted me completely. And I valued that trust immensely.

The final point of leadership that I learned from Mr. Turner was the importance of caring about people. *He cared about people, and he cared about me!* It is essential to understand that he modeled what he taught. Mr. Turner was a strong Christian. He loved people, and it showed. I remember times when someone came into the store hungry and asked Mr. Turner for money. Many alcoholics wandered the downtown area where the store was located, so Mr. Turner was wise not to give anyone money. But he would offer them food and something to drink. He never sent someone away who was hungry. He always dealt fairly with others, paying his bills on time and going the extra mile when someone had a complaint. And I was one of those people he cared about. He cared about things in my life: how school was going, who I was dating, how things were at home. He was a great listener, which reflected how much he cared.

So what are some of the keys to being a good leader? First, learn to be a good listener. You might ask: "How do I do that?" The answer is simple: talk less and listen more. When I listen, I try to look into the eyes of the person I am listening to. I will break into the conversation to clarify and confirm what I am hearing, so the other person knows I am really listening and not daydreaming. And I try to listen with the goal of learning. Sometimes I catch myself in a conversation in which I am planning what to say next rather than really listening to what someone is telling me. That is not being a good listener. That is tuning out what someone else is saying in order to make sure you get your point across. James 1:19-20 says:

> *My dear brothers, take note of this: Everyone should be quick to listen, slow to speak, and slow to become angry, for man's anger does not bring about the righteous life that God desires.*

The second key of being a good leader, which ties in with being a good listener, is letting others know that you care about them. This cannot be "pretending to care"; it must be genuine or else you will lose credibility very quickly. Others know that you care about them when you can empathize and sympathize with them. There will be times when they need a hug. And there will be times when they need you to tactfully tell them what they do not want to hear. But they appreciate it because you have built that relationship with them, and they know you really care about them.

The third key to being a good leader is to have a teachable spirit and be patient as you are teaching others. Make sure you are spending time in God's Word, learning and growing in your faith. By doing this, you will live your life in a way that people will be attracted to your faith; they will want the peace that you have.

Finally, you need to find two special men in your life. You need to find someone who can be a mentor to you, and you need to find someone to whom you can be a mentor, someone in whom you can invest your time and life. Your mentor may not be a great speaker or have a college degree. He simply needs to be someone you can learn from and someone who can help you grow beyond your comfort zone. Likewise, as you have the opportunity to help someone else as their mentor, be patient, listen carefully, encourage them, and be sure to let them know you really care about them. Remember that others are watching you and learning from you even when you are unaware.

---

# Leadership

*Father God, I pray for the man who is reading this who recognizes he is a leader and that others are watching him. I pray for Your strength and guidance. Please help him to be authentic. I pray he will make wise choices, and when he fails, give him the humility to admit those failures. Give him Your wisdom, knowledge, and abilities.*

*I pray for the one who needs a leader and mentor to come into his life. I pray, Father, that you would bring the right mentor into his life. Bring someone in to his life that can encourage him, teach him, and help him recognize how much You love him.*

*I pray You will help each of us grow in our knowledge of You. Help us to truly care about others we come in contact with each day. Forgive us for the opportunities we have missed to demonstrate Your love and care to others in need.*

*Thank You for Your extraordinary love. Amen.*

## Questions to Ponder

1) How would you define leadership? Do you believe this is something innate or something learned?

2) Who would you say epitomizes the qualities of great leadership today? What was it about them that made them such a good leaders? How have they influenced your life?

3) If you were describing yourself, would you say you were more of a leader or more of a follower? Why? How do you think your best friend would describe you?

4) What do you think God wants you to be: a leader, a follower, or both? Why?

5) If you believe God expects you to take on leadership roles at times, what specific steps will you take to improve your leadership skills? (Do you know of training courses or books that would be helpful? Are there opportunities for "on-the-job training" where you could begin to lead someone who needs some godly leadership?)

# Leadership

List some specific steps now that you will take to help yourself grow in this area.

_____
_____
_____
_____
_____
_____
_____
_____
_____
_____
_____

## Chapter 9

# Timeless Goals

*"Your attitude, not your aptitude, determines your altitude."*[1]
*- Zig Ziglar*

---

I believe in goal-setting. In fact, I believe everyone should have short-term goals of things they want to accomplish within the next twelve months, medium-range goals that span the next five years, and lifetime goals of things they want to achieve while they are on this earth. You may have heard the famous quote: "If you don't know where you're going, any road will take you there." Let me be more direct: I believe that it will be almost impossible to accomplish anything significant without setting personal goals.

Goals can be like walking into an ice-cream shop; there are many varieties to choose from, and some turn out good, whereas others leave a lot to be desired. Setting goals can be harmful if you set the bar so high that they are not achievable and leads to frustration and depression. For example, if I had set as my personal goal to become a star quarterback in the NFL, and I made that my life's dream, I would have spent a lot of energy and time for nothing. I simply do not have the body or the skills to be an NFL quarterback, and no amount of work or training would change that. Similarly, I could desire to become an astronaut and go to the moon and make that a lifetime goal. But the truth is that such a dream is unrealistic for me at this stage of my life unless the requirements for leaving this atmosphere radically change in my lifetime. So it is essential that you set *realistic* goals.

In addition to setting realistic goals, it is vital to set *important* goals. To me, an important goal is one that will have an impact on me, on my family, or on others around me. For example, writing this book is important to me, but hopefully, it will be meaningful to my three sons and positively influence others who may read it. Another of my personal goals is to take a foreign mission trip. I want to be able to share God's love with a people-group that has never heard of Jesus and what He did for them. This is an important goal for me because it could make an eternal impact on the lives of many others and future generations.

When it comes to setting goals, the first thing many people think about is a financial goal. For example, someone may set a goal of making a million dollars. In his famous book *The Goal*, Eli Goldratt says the primary goal of every business must be to make money.[2] While this is certainly true for businesses, I believe it falls short of being a key goal for individuals. I am not saying that there is anything wrong with having healthy financial goals or desiring to make a million dollars, but my question would be, "for what reason?" If you achieve this goal, what then? Do you remember the story about the Mexican fisherman? The dream of becoming financially well-off so he could retire to the fishing village to spend time with his family did not make a lot of sense. The real goal for him was to spend time with his family – something he was already doing in his current job.

It is critical as you set goals that you understand the reason for the goal and what its achievement really means. For example, it may be appropriate to have a goal of making a million dollars so that you could give to a worthy cause such as feeding the poor or helping spread the gospel. If the goal involves saving for retirement to ensure you and your wife do not have to depend on anyone else, that is a worthy goal (and one more people should take seriously). But if the goal has only selfish motives – buying more "toys" or more indulgences, you might want to reconsider the value of the goal and its appropriateness.

So how do you set goals? I would recommend that you plan a time where you can get by yourself, free from all distractions. This should be at least an hour and perhaps as much as a whole day. Consider the setting. Maybe you have a favorite place you like to go – a quiet place by a waterfall or a view of the mountains. Perhaps it is a visit to the beach where you can hear nothing but the sound of the waves. Wherever it is, make a plan. This is Step One – *make a plan*.

Once you have planned a time and place, the second step is to *begin to pray*. Ask God to help you in setting appropriate goals for your life. Ask Him to help you identify some things that He wants you to do, significant things, things that are good uses of the time, talents, and resources He has blessed you with, or that He will bless you with in the future. You may also consider fasting during this time. If so, do some homework on proper fasting so that you do it safely. Find some resources that can guide you. You may want to consult with your doctor about this. Improper fasting can result in serious health issues.

The third step is to *write*. When the time comes to actually begin setting your goals, make sure you have a way to write down your thoughts. Begin with a brainstorming exercise where you spend at least thirty minutes just writing down possibilities of things you would like to do in life. Write down whatever comes to mind. Perhaps it is learning to play the piano or running a marathon. Maybe it is learning to ski. Perhaps it is visiting a foreign country that you have always wanted to see. Write down anything that comes to mind.

When you finish the initial brainstorm, take time to ask God for guidance and go back through your list. Now there is nothing wrong with any of the things I have mentioned above. They are all legal. They are morally neutral. They are perfectly legitimate goals. But they may be secondary goals. That is, they may be things that bring you enjoyment or relaxation, and that is fine. But there should also be some things that have eternal value among the list.

Primary goals should have an eternal purpose in mind. If you do not find any goals that fall in this category, brainstorm some more with eternity in focus. We are stewards of the time God has given us, and our goals should be aligned with His will for our life. Identify at least one one-year goal, one five-year goal, and one lifetime goal with an eternal purpose. Then list as many secondary goals as you wish. Go back through the secondary goals and see if any of them could be tied to something with eternal value. For example, let's say you had as a goal going on an African safari. You might look at this and think about how to tie this in with a mission trip to share the gospel with a people-group that has never heard the good news.

These goals are "whats" or possibilities, which means they represent what you would like to do someday. When you finish identifying your list of "whats," go back and add a column for "when." Then go back through the list one more time and make a note of "how." Going back to our example of visiting Africa, you will need to look at how you will get enough time off work, how you will save the money or raise funds to make the trip, and consider all the other essential factors. This is a crucial step because you must make a plan of action before you can realize your goals. This is the last step – *plan a course of action*.

| **What** | **When** | **How** |
|---|---|---|
| Play piano | Fall 2008 | Find local teacher |
| Foreign Mission Trip (Russia) | 2010 | Save two weeks vacation; set aside funds in 2009 & 2010 |
| Dance lessons with wife | Begin Fall 2008 | Find local training |
| Record Christian Music CD from songs written | 2012 | Talk with local artist (ML & JP); set aside funds in 2011 |
| Annual Beach House with kids & their families | Annually | Set aside funds for a larger house as part of the budget |
| Read through the entire Bible | Annually | Follow the "One Year Bible" plan, reading each morning before work |

There is a caution I must share before closing this chapter, and it is crucial. Listen carefully: God has the right to disrupt our plans, our goals, and our lives. This does not mean that God is a cruel God or that He does not want what is best for us. On the contrary, in Jeremiah 29:11, God says:

> *For I know the plans I have for you, declares the Lord, plans to prosper you and not to harm you, plans to give you hope and a future.*

It is essential to realize that God has a plan for our lives, but our plans do not always align with His. Remember that Joseph was sold into slavery in the book of Genesis, and it was many years later before he became second in command in Egypt. God dramatically disrupted Joseph's life. And in the end, Joseph recognized that even though his brothers intended evil, God had a plan which was good. Joseph accepted God's sovereignty in his life. He also accepted the fact that God does not operate on the same timetable that we have. Even though Joseph suffered for many years, he still recognized that his life and his time belonged to God.

Consider Abraham who had to leave the comforts of city life to wander as a nomad when God called him. Abraham did not know where God was leading him, and when he arrived, it may have been different than what he expected. But it was exactly as God had planned it. So we must recognize God can disrupt our plans, and we need to be okay with that. Sometimes we may understand why. For other circumstances, we may not understand it until we get to heaven.

When I was in my late teenage years, I wanted to be President of the United States. (You can stop laughing now). Seriously, I wanted to be President, even though I did nothing to prepare myself for such a role, nor did I have a timetable in mind. It was sort of a mental dream, but not a purposeful, intentional goal with actions around it. If it had been a serious goal, I would have prepared myself in college to enter politics. I would have probably run for a local office like the School Board or County Council. I would have worked my way up to the State Legislature and then possibly Governor or Senator. At that point, I would have been prepared to make a run for the Presidency. But the path I took gave me no preparation for such an office. It was never a serious goal. I had not planned a "how" or a "when." It was simply an empty dream. So my challenge to you is to put on paper goals that you plan to take seriously. Dream big, and be intentional about preparing yourself to achieve those goals. Pray about them and ask God to help you accomplish them according to His will. And if God redirects your path so that some of them cannot be realized, thank Him for closing those doors and look for the new windows of opportunity He may be opening.

---

*Father God, I pray for the one who is considering setting goals for the first time in his life. I know it can be overwhelming to think about long-term goals, whether you are young or old. I ask for Your guidance in setting goals with an eternal purpose. I pray You will bring to mind those things You want each of us to accomplish. I believe You have put us here on earth to accomplish Your plans and purposes, and I ask that You reveal those to each of us.*

*And most of all, I know You desire us to worship You. I pray that You would help us have that close intimate relationship with You and make our primary goal to worship You in our hearts with all sincerity. Help us to glorify You with our lives, both with the goals we set and with the way we love life each day.*

*You tell us in Your Word that there is time for everything. And I pray You would help us find the balance between times of work, times of pleasure, and times of reaching the lost for You. Thank You for Your great love. In Jesus' name I pray. Amen.*

## Questions to Ponder

1) Have you ever set any serious goals for yourself — ones that had a timetable and a way in which you planned to accomplish them? Describe how you set about defining these. Did you pray and ask God for guidance and direction as you set your goals? Have you achieved any of them yet? Why or why not?

2) What is the biggest obstacle that prevents you from setting goals? Is it just a matter of discipline, of spending the time to map out a plan? Or is it something else?

3) Will you commit to setting at least one one-year goal, one five-year goal, and one lifetime goal? What is your timetable for clearly defining these goals and writing them down?

4) Who will you share your goals with so that they can help hold you accountable?

5) Are you prepared for God to disrupt your plans? What will it mean if your plans are significantly disrupted?

## Chapter 10

# Final Thoughts

*"All men are like grass, and all their glory is like the flowers of the field; the grass withers and the flowers fall, but the word of the Lord stands forever."*
*I Peter 1:24-25*

---

If an angel appeared to you this morning and told you today would be the last day of your life, what would you do today? I doubt it would be an ordinary day of taking a shower and going to work. I doubt you would go to the golf course to play one last round. You probably would not sit on your couch in front of the television watching your favorite show one last time. My guess is that you would begin by thinking about things you need to make right before your time expires. Maybe it is a phone call that you have needed to make for a long time. Or perhaps it is someone you need to go to and have a serious face-to-face conversation. For some, you would spend the entire day with your wife and children, even though you had not done that in a very long time.

Here is my final encouragement: live your life in such a way that when you lay down each night, you are at peace — at peace with yourself, at peace with the world, at peace with God. Romans 12:18 says: *"If it is possible, as far as it depends on you, live at peace with everyone."* And in James 3:17-18, the Bible says:

> *But the wisdom that comes from heaven is first of all pure; then peace-loving, considerate, submissive, full of mercy and good fruit, impartial and sincere. Peacemakers who sow in peace raise a harvest of righteousness.*

I believe to be genuinely at peace, we must frequently ask ourselves questions like:

- Am I harboring any unforgiveness?
- Is there anyone that I need to ask for forgiveness?
- Have I done everything in my power to be at peace with everyone I know?
- Are my priorities right? Is God first in my life? Is my family second place in my life?
- Have I been a good steward of the time and money God has entrusted to me?
- Are my debts and my investments appropriate so that they cause me no worry?
- If I die tonight in my sleep and stand before the Lord to give an account of my life, am I prayed up? Have I confessed every sin that I am aware of?
- Am I living my life in a way that will please God?

I believe it is important to make time for self-assessment and reflection about how we are living our lives. That is the message I have tried to communicate in *FATHERLY ADVICE ~ BUILDING CHARACTER*.

Hopefully, I have given you some questions to ask when you are making your own evaluation and some potential ways to improve your life and your relationships. In the final analysis, life is not about things; it is about relationships. It is about how we relate to God, to our family, and to others around us.

An unknown author wrote:

> *I stood on the streets of a busy town*
> *Watching men tearing a building down;*
> *With a 'ho, heave, ho,' and a lusty yell,*
> *They swung a beam, and a sidewall fell.*
> *I asked the foreman: 'Are those men as skilled,*
> *The kind you'd hire if you wanted to build?'*
> *'Ah, no,' he said, 'no, indeed.*
> *Just a common laborer is all I need.*
> *I can tear down as much in a day or two*
> *What it would take skilled men a year to do.*
> *And then I thought as I went on my way,*
> *Just which of these roles am I trying to play?*
> *Have I walked life's road with scriptural care,*
> *Measuring each deed with rule and square?*
> *Or am I of those who roam the town*
> *Content with the labor of tearing down?"*

Remember, life is a journey. We will not reach our destination until this life is over. So pedal hard up the steep hills of life, taking time to catch the view when you reach the top. Take a breath as you come down the backside, watching out for the unexpected curves and falling rocks. Keep your balance, which is sometimes tricky. And most importantly, enjoy the ride. You only have one life to live!

*F*ather God, I thank You for loving each of us with an incredible love that we can never fully understand. Thank You for giving me the words to write in this book, and I pray You will use them to encourage and truly transform the lives of each one who is reading this. I pray for the reader who does not know You as Lord and Savior. I ask You to draw him to Yourself and give him the courage to find out how he can have eternal life with You. I pray You would help each of us live our lives growing in our relationships and caring for our fellow man. And may our lives reflect Your love to everyone around us, knowing that we may be the only Jesus some will ever see. I offer all of this up to You in the name of Jesus. Amen.

## Questions to Ponder

1) Are you at peace with yourself? If not, why not? What would have to happen for you to be at peace? If your answer is not within your control, are you letting others determine your peace?

2) If you believe the most important things in life are relationships, what are you doing to grow your relationship with God? With your wife? With your children? With others?

3) What is the one thing you will do in response to reading this book? Make it specific and with a timetable.

4) If you were seeking some *FATHERLY ADVICE*, what is the one question you would like to ask? Feel free to send me your questions at: george.wofford@gmail.com

# Appendix:
# Grace Through Faith

*"For it is by grace you have been saved, through faith – and this not from yourselves, it is the gift of God – not by works, so that no one can boast."*
Ephesians 2:8-9

---

If you do not have a personal relationship with Jesus Christ, I would love to introduce you to Him. I want you to know something that is very important: *God loves you!* He really does. The Bible tells us in First Timothy 2:3-4 that God *"wants all men to be saved and to come to a knowledge of the truth."* Perhaps you have always believed that God will not let anyone go to Hell, and in the end, He will let everyone into Heaven. There is a problem with that type of thinking. It assumes things about God that do not line up with His Word. There is one thing that separates us from God – do you know what that is? It is sin.

Sin describes the things in our lives that violate God's commands. Have you ever told a lie? Have you ever stolen anything? Have you ever wanted something that belonged to someone else? Have you ever used God's name carelessly, perhaps cursing someone or something? Have you ever had evil thoughts that you allowed your mind to dwell on? Have you ever lusted after a woman that was not your wife? Have you ever wanted revenge after being mistreated?

*Everyone sins.* Romans 3:23 says, *"For all have sinned and fall short of the glory of God."* Every human being except Jesus Christ has sinned. And it is this sin that destroyed our relationship with God. Our sin prevents us from being in God's presence now and for all eternity. Romans 6:23 says, *"For the wages of sin is death...."* That is not just physical death; it is spiritual death and everlasting death – permanent separation from God. Wages are what we earn; it is what we deserve based on our actions (sin!). But there is *good news.*

Jesus Christ came to earth to take our punishment. When He was crucified on a Roman cross two thousand years ago, He chose to die for our sins. He took our place and offered Himself as the ultimate sacrifice for all of mankind's sin. Jesus was the only one who could take our punishment because He was the only person who ever lived who was sinless. He was (and is) pure and holy. He was God in a human body. And because of His sacrifice, He offers His free gift of grace to anyone who will make Him Lord of their life. But that is the catch. In order for Jesus Christ to take your punishment, you have to be willing to *confess that you are a sinner, believe that Jesus Christ came to die for your sins, and make Him Lord of your life.*

There is a story of a famous tightrope walker who had stretched a rope between two skyscrapers in New York. A great crowd gathered to watch him cross. He skillfully maneuvered his way across with thunderous applause from the audience as he reached the other side. He then took a wheelbarrow with 200 pounds of sand and pushed it back across the rope again to thunderous applause. He asked his audience, "How many of you believe I can push this wheelbarrow full of 200 pounds back across the rope?" The crowd went wild as everyone chanted, "I believe you can, I believe you can!" The tightrope walker then dumped the sand out of the wheelbarrow and asked, "Who will be the first one willing to climb into this wheelbarrow?"

That is what Jesus means when He says we must believe – we must be willing to get into the wheelbarrow and let Christ lead us through this life. Are you ready to do that? If so, let me encourage you to pray something like this:

*F**ather God,*
*I recognize that I am a sinner. I have lived my life pleasing myself all these years. I ask Your forgiveness for my sin. Your Word promises that if we confess our sin, You will forgive us and cleanse us from all our unrighteousness. I want to be in a right relationship with You, and I am ready to make You Lord of my life. Help me to grow in my faith as I begin reading the Bible. Thank You for Your forgiveness and for giving me eternal life with You. I ask this in Jesus' name. Amen.*

If you sincerely prayed this prayer, your sins are forgiven. God wrote your name in a special book, called the Book of Life, which He will open at the end of time. You are listed now as one of His children. John 1:12 says, "*Yet to all who received him, to those who believed in his name, he gave the right to become children of God.*" You will live forever with Him, and nothing can change that. You will always be His child from this day forward. You will begin to enjoy His blessings on your life, and you will have joy and peace that you have never experienced before.

That does not mean you will have an easy life. It does not mean all your problems will disappear. It does not mean broken relationships from the past will be instantly healed. Life will still be challenging at times. There is still evil in the world, and Satan will try to tempt you or attack you. But you can be sure that God will never leave you. He is now on your side because you belong to Him. Nothing can strip you of your right to be God's child. Romans 8:38-39 says

> *For I am convinced that neither death nor life, neither angels nor demons, neither the present nor the future, nor any powers, neither height nor depth, nor anything else in all creation, will be able to separate us from the love of God that is in Christ Jesus our Lord*

If you prayed this prayer, I would love to hear from you. Please feel free to send me an e-mail at george.wofford@gmail.com

The next step is to find a local church in which you can become active. Find some other Christians with whom you can begin to develop a friendship. Remember above all that God loves you, and He has a plan for your life. May God bless you as you grow in your knowledge of Him and as He begins to change your life in remarkable ways.

# Endnotes

## Introduction

1. Gary Smalley and John Trent, *the Gift of the Blessing*, (New York, NY: Inspirational Press, 1998), 37-54.

2. Robert Lewis, *Raising A Modern Day Knight*, (Wheaton, Illinois, 1997: Tyndale House Publishers), 97-136.

## Chapter 1 – Priorities

1. Corrie ten Boom, *The Hiding Place*, (Minneapolis, MN: World Wide Publications, 1971), 26-27.

2. Gary Ezzo and Anne Marie Ezzo, *Growing Kid's God's Way*, 4th Edition (Chatsworth, California: Growing Families International Press, 1993), 103-120.

3. Harry Chapin, *Verities and Balderdash*: "Cats in the Cradle," (Electra Records, 1974)

4. Gary Ezzo and Anne Marie Ezzo, *Growing Kid's God's Way*, 4th Edition (Chatsworth, California: Growing Families International Press, 1993), 272.

5. Henry B. Eyring, *"Child of Promise"* (Speeches, Brigham Young University; 218 University Press Building, Provo, Utah, 1986).

## Chapter 2 – Faithfulness

1. *Holy Bible, New International Version*, (Grand Rapids, Michigan: Zondervan Publishing House, 1984), Psalm 119:11.

2. Kay Arthur, *How to Study Your Bible*, (Eugene, Oregon: Harvest House Publishers, 1994).

3. Charles M. Sheldon, *In His Steps, What would Jesus Do?*, (Uhrichsville, Ohio: Barbour Publishing, 1996).

4. *Holy Bible, New International Version*, (Grand Rapids, Michigan: Zondervan Publishing House, 1984), Second Peter 2:7.

## Chapter 3 – Patience

1. Helen Keller, "Laura Moncur's Motivational Quotations." The Quotations Page. 2007. 20 Jan 2008 <http://www.Quotationspage.com>.

2. The Holy Bible: King James Version. (Iowa Falls, IA: World Bible Publishers, 2001).

3. Holy Bible, New International Version, (Grand Rapids, Michigan: Zondervan Publishing House, 1984), Psalm 119:105.

## Chapter 4 – Forgiveness

1. Philip Yancey, What's so Amazing about Grace?, (Grand Rapids, Michigan: Zondervan, 1997), p. 100

2. Corrie ten Boom and Jamie Buckingham, Tramp for the Lord, (Grand Rapids, Michigan: Fleming H. Revell Company, 1974), 181-183.

## Chapter 5 – Integrity

1. Charles M. Sheldon, In *His Steps, What would Jesus Do?*, (Uhrichsville, Ohio: Barbour Publishing, 1996).

### Chapter 6 - Love

1. Gary Chapman, The Five Love Languages, (Chicago: Northfield Publishing, 1995), 24.

### Chapter 7 - Accountability

1. Steve Farrar, Point Man, (Sisters, Oregon: Multnomah Publishers, Inc., 2003), 141.

### Chapter 8 - Leadership

1. Woodrow Wilson, "Laura Moncur's Motivational Quotations." The Quotations Page. 2007. 20 Jan 2008 <http://www.Quotationspage.com>.

### Chapter 9 – The Goal

1. Zig Ziglar, "Zig Ziglar." Wikipedia. 2008. Wikipedia, The Free Encyclopedia. 4 Feb 2008. <http://en.wikipedia.org/w/index.php?title=Zig_Ziglar&oldid=188954246 >.

2. Eliyahu Goldratt and Jeff Cox, The Goal, (Great Barrington, Massachusetts: North River Press, 1992), 40.

www.ingramcontent.com/pod-product-compliance
Lightning Source LLC
LaVergne TN
LVHW011422080426
835512LV00005B/211